CHRIS R. MANUEL

Twilight Lubang

THE #1 NEW YORK TIMES BEST SELLER

A PATH IN THE JUNGLE

TWILIGHT
LUBANG

———

CHRIS R. MANUEL
Twilight
Lubang
THE #1 NEW YORK TIMES BEST SELLER
A PATH IN THE JUNGLE

Copyright © Chris R. Manuel
All rights Reserved

ISBN: 978-5-5208-0912-8

Lubang, a Path in the Jungle

February 20, 1974

The night curls in fever dreams. No sooner conscious than with a
horrendous shiver, the scene uncovers itself as a solid daytime
variant of a similar bad dream, popping and gleaming like
inexactly associated neon tubes. From dawn the wilderness has
jerked in the ceremonial torments of power. Downpour. The
tempest is far off to such an extent that its thunder isn't yet
perceptible. A fantasy? Is it a fantasy? A wide way, on either
side thick underbrush, decaying mulch on the ground, the leaves
trickling. The wilderness stays solid, patient, humble, until the
workplace of the downpour has been commended.
Then, at that point, this, like I'd been there myself. Hints of
voices somewhere far off; blissful cries drawing ever closer.
From the insubstantial fog of the wilderness a body gains
structure. A youthful Filipino man comes picking up the pace the
way, down the slight slope. Inquisitive, as he runs, in one hand
he holds up over his head the remainders of an umbrella,
presently only a wire skeleton and smidgens of fabric, in the
other a bolo blade. Not far behind him is a lady with a baby on
her arm, trailed by seven or eight different townspeople. What
has incited the blissful fervor isn't clear. They hustle by, then
nothing occurs. The consistent trickle, dribble from the trees, the
tranquil way.
A way, simply a wilderness trail. But, preceding me, on the
right-hand side, a mix goes through a couple of the disintegrating
leaves. What was that? One more snapshot of tranquility. Then a
part of the mass of leaves at eye level before me, that also starts
to move. Gradually, frightfully leisurely, a green man takes
structure. Is it a phantom? What I have been observing from the
start without remembering it is a Japanese trooper. Hiroo Onoda.
Regardless of whether I had known precisely where he was

standing, I could never have seen him, so consummate is his disguise. He strips the wet leaves off his legs, then the green twigs he has painstakingly affixed to his body. He ventures into the shrubbery for his rifle, alongside which he has hidden his disguised backpack. I see a tactical man in his mid fifties; a wiry form; each development exaggeratedly watchful. His uniform is made of sewn-together pieces; the knob of his rifle is twisted around with tree covering. He listens eagerly, then vanishes quietly after the townspeople. In front of me is the dirt way, as yet unchanged, yet new now, unique, brimming with mysteries. Was it a fantasy?

The way, a little lower presently, has enlarged out as of now. The downpour is something like a stream. Onoda concentrates on the impressions in the earth, listening constantly, continually on the alarm. His enthusiastic eyes turn toward each path. The birds have struck up, tranquilly, like to guarantee him that peril is a word in a word reference now, a strange state of the scene. The murmuring of the bugs is customary. I begin to hear with Onoda's ears that their murmuring isn't forceful, isn't grieved. From a far distance the pouring of a stream, despite the fact that I still can't seem to see a stream, like I were, as Onoda, starting to decipher sounds.

Lubang, Wakayama Tributary

February 21, 1974

As of now, the clerestory of the backwoods has congested a thin creek. Clear water pours over level stones. A subsequent stream goes along with it from the left, plunging from steep lush slopes. Past the juncture of the two, the scene broadens out, smooths. Bamboo, palms, tall surges. At the actual conjunction there is a level shoal. Onoda crosses the sand strolling in reverse, passing on follows to deceive a potential follower. Through the gradually influencing surges he can make out a little Japanese banner. Onoda warily raises his field glasses, worn and set apart by such countless years in the wilderness. Could it be said that they are as a matter of fact actually field glasses? Weren't the crystals quite a while in the past went after by a shape? Or then again is Onoda difficult to envision without his handle glasses? The banner folds a little in the early evening breeze. Its texture is new to the point that the wrinkles where it was collapsed are still plainly perceptible.
There is a tent close to the banner. It, as well, straight from the manufacturing plant, the kind of tent travelers could use for an end of the week outing. Onoda circumspectly fixes up. He sees a young fellow hunching down on the ground, confronting ceaselessly, attempting to get a fire rolling in a camp oven. Obviously alone. A nylon backpack in the mouth of the tent. At the point when the young fellow goes to go after it to make a windbreak close to the cooker, his face shows: it is Norio Suzuki.

Onoda jumps forward from his trap. Suzuki is inflexible with dread, sees the rifle pointing at him. It takes him a second to recuperate the force of discourse.
"I'm Japanese," he says, "I'm Japanese."

"Kneeling down," orders Onoda. Suzuki gradually gets kneeling down.

"Take your shoes off. Discard them to the furthest extent that you would be able."

Suzuki follows the order, he is shaking so hard he experiences difficulty with the bands.

"I'm unarmed," he says. "This is only a kitchen blade."

Onoda pays no respect to the blade on the ground. Suzuki cautiously drives it away.

"Is it safe to say that you are Onoda? Hiroo Onoda?"

"Indeed. Lieutenant Onoda. That is me."

Onoda focuses his rifle at the center of Suzuki's chest, indifferent, hazy. Presently liveliness comes over Suzuki's highlights.

"Am I dreaming? Am I truly seeing the way things are playing out?"

Sunlight has given approach to night. Onoda and Suzuki are crouching by the fire somewhat way away from Suzuki's tent. Nighttime crickets start their droning. Onoda has taken up a situation from where he can overview the environmental factors with his constantly turning respect. He is dubious, alert, his rifle actually pointed in the overall course of Suzuki. It appears they probably been representing some time. After stopping for a moment, Suzuki takes up the discussion.

"How is it that I could be an American specialist? I'm just 22 years of age."

Onoda isn't intrigued. "I was more experienced than you at least a year, by the time i arrived at the beginning conflict. Any work to avoid me from my main goal was crafted by foe specialists."

"I'm not your adversary. My main design was to meet you."

"Non-military persons dressed on their vests came onboard on the island. Men in mask. They generally needed exactly the same thing: to kill me or take me prisoner. I have endure 111 ambushes. I have been more than once gone after. I can never again count how frequently I was terminated upon. Each individual on this island is my adversary."

Suzuki has no response. Onoda glances off the way of the last light overhead.

"Do you have in light like this any knowledge how a shot projectile looks like?"

"No. I can't say I do."

"It has a somewhat blue shine, practically like tracer."

"Truly?"

"You can visualize it coming in front of you, supposed if it was terminated very far from you."

"What's more, you weren't hit?" Suzuki asks, in perplexity.

"I would have been hit. I turned aside, and the slug went past me."

"Do shots whistle as they fly?"

"No, yet they make a kind of vibration. A low buzz."

Suzuki is dazzled.

Another voice participates. There's a far off glinting in the night sky. The new voice is singing something.

"Who's there?" Suzuki can't make anybody out.

"That would be Shimada, Corporal Shimada. He passed on here."

"However, wasn't that in the center fifties? I read about it. Everybody in Japan is familiar with it."

"He was dead at least 19years, 9months,and 14days before now. We were trapped here, by the Wakayama feeder."

"Wakayama?" asks Suzuki. "Sounds Japanese."

"Right toward the start of our main goal on Lubang, my regiment picked this name for the feeder, out of appreciation for my local prefecture, Wakayama."

The crickets are stronger, filling the scene with their clamor. The discussion is all theirs now. Suzuki thinks for quite a while. At last, every one of the crickets shout out on the double, in some aggregate resentment.

"Onoda-san?"

"Lieutenant."

"Lieutenant, we are apparently circumventing around and around."

Suzuki is quiet. Onoda nudges Suzuki in the chest with the rifle, not threateningly, yet to ensure he makes all the difference for the discharge.

"Assuming you're no adversary specialist, who are you?"

"I am Norio Suzuki. I used to be an understudy at Tokyo University."

"Used to be?"

"I quit."

"No understudy at the best college in the nation stops."

"I was annoyed in light of the fact that I could see my entire future delineated in front of me, constantly to retirement and annuity."

"Well?" Onoda doesn't have any idea.

"I was in need of years of opportunity, before i became a being of money manager, forfeiting my life."

"Well?"

"I began to travel. I bummed a ride. I've been to forty nations."

"What is this — catching a ride?"

"Waving to vehicles, trusting they get you and take you any place they're going. No unique objective. Until I arrived."

"Where?"

"Really, I had three points. The first was to track down you, Lieutenant Onoda."

"Nobody tracks down me. In 29 years nobody has tracked down me."

Suzuki feels empowered.

"I have been hanging around for under two days, and I have tracked down you."

"I coincidentally found you, I tracked down you. You didn't track down me. On the off chance that you hadn't been so crazy as to risk, I would presumably have killed you."

Suzuki has not anticipated this. He is quiet.

"Furthermore, what were your two different goals?"

"The sasquatch — "

"Who?"

"Some of the time called the accursed snowman. A horrendous animal in the Himalayas, shrouded in fur. They have found hints of him, he exists. And afterward the goliath panda right at home in the mountains in China. In a specific order: Onoda, sasquatch, panda."

Interestingly, there's a glint of entertainment all over. He gestures to Suzuki, go on, don't stop.

Suzuki feels empowered. "At a very long time the conflict ended."

Utter bland incomprehension from Onoda.

"That can't be."

"Japan gave in August 1945."

"The conflict isn't finished. Two or three days prior, I saw an American plane carrying warship, joined by a destroyer and a frigate."

"Traveling East, I anticipate," says Suzuki.

"Try not to attempt to deceive me. I see what I see."

Suzuki stays tenacious.

"Lieutenant, the US maritime have their greatest base in Subic Bay. All their naval force ships are refitted and prepared there."

"The Bay of Manila? That is just ninety kilometers away."

"Indeed."

"That base existed toward the start of the conflict. How do American ships currently come and use it?"

"The US and the Philippines are partners."

"Shouldn't something be said about the planes, the contenders and aircraft, I see them constantly?"
"They're set out toward Clark Air Base, North of the Bay of Manila. With such enormous powers, Lieutenant, is there any good reason why the adversary wouldn't just invade Lubang? All things considered, Lubang controls admittance to the Bay of Manila."
"I'm not conscious of the foe's arrangements."
"There are no more plans, the conflict is finished."
Onoda battles with himself briefly. Then leisurely he gets to his feet, moves toward Suzuki, and presses the gag of his rifle against his temple.
"Okay, come clean with me. The opportunity has arrived."
"Lieutenant, I am not scared of passing on. Yet, it would be hopeless to be killed for coming clean."

The night turns into the longest evening, a shock for Onoda, who is torn all over among uncertainty and acknowledgment. There is no apparent indication of this, his face stays stony. Nuclear bombs dropped on two Japanese urban communities, that's what a hundred thousand dead very much like? Something about the energy let out of the parting of iotas, made into a weapon. How? Suzuki misses the mark on mechanical comprehension to make sense of it. Different nations had at this point likewise gained this thing, this nuclear bomb. The current armory was perfect to the point that it could kill each occupant of the earth more than once, yet multiple times. For Onoda, this isn't viable with the rationale of any conflict he can imagine, not even from now on.

What had occurred later — supposedly — the two bombs had fallen on Japan is what Onoda needs to be aware. It was August 1945. Japan had abdicated genuinely. The Emperor had tended to his kin over the remote. Nobody had heard his voice. He had made a move to proclaim that he was not a divine being. Such a declaration is so unfathomable to Onoda that he accepts it as definite confirmation that Suzuki has come determined to mislead him. He penetrates the gag of the rifle between Suzuki's eyes.

"No. Actually the conflict has gone on. Maybe it just continued somewhere else."

However, Suzuki stays resolute. "In the West, Germany lost. They gave up before the Japanese did."

"No," says Onoda, "the conflict went on, and it happened in the West too. What I saw is verification."

"Confirmation? What do you intend to say, 'verification'?"

"I saw plenty of American warplanes flying above. Here, going that way, West."

"When was this?"

"It happened for a really long time."

"Starting when?"

"In 1950. Likewise planes and troop carriers, maritime boats."

"That was the Korean War."

"Korean War? What Korean War? Korea has a place with us."

"The Communists tossed out the Japanese. Then, at that point, the US began a conflict with the Communists."

"Also, America obviously lost."

"Half won, half lost. Today, Korea has been apportioned. There is a Communist North and a Capitalist South."

Onoda is finding it challenging to process such a lot of data.

"In any case, those floods of warplanes, they won't ever stop."

"What warplanes? When?"

"Continuously going West. American aircraft straightforwardly above. Increasingly more constantly. From 1965, in immense developments. Entire guards of boats, greater constantly, increasingly more of them. Also, you're attempting to tell me, the conflict has finished?"

"That was the Vietnam War."

"The what?"

Onoda reclines. The night is long. The crickets, not thinking often about war or harmony, or who will name wars and why, heighten their dull shouting, this is their conflict, maybe additionally their tranquility talks, similarly unbeknownst to us. The moon. The early light of the approaching day makes it still paler, a superb body with next to no more profound significance that has been around for a long period of time before there were any people.

Like following some quiet getting it, Onoda and Suzuki gaze toward it at indeed the very same time. "Men have arrived on the moon," Suzuki says delicately, like hesitant to express too many stunning things excessively fast.
"When? How?"
"Over the most recent five years. The groups flew in rockets and space containers. I'm opposed to say as much, however the space explorers were Americans, our previous adversaries."
"America is as yet our adversary."
"Not actually. They even went to our Olympic Games."
"I am familiar with those Games," says Onoda.
"In what manner or capacity?" asks Suzuki.
"Adversary specialists left out duplicates of painstakingly manufactured Japanese papers in different places all around the island. A few pieces of them even looked solid, yet the main place of them was to bait me out of the wilderness." Onoda stops, considers. "I will continue with my conflict. I have been battling for a very long time as of now, and I have a lot more years left in me."
"In any case, those realities I had the option to fill you in about — "

"I'll consider it," Onoda hinders him.
"How can you end your mission, what does it take?" Suzuki asks delicately.
Onoda mulls over everything.

"That large number of flyers dropped from planes moving
toward me to surrender — they were all fakes, I can show it."
He says it more to himself than to his startling guest.
"There is just a single condition on which I would give up. Only
one."
"Also, what might that be?" asks Suzuki.
"Assuming that one of my bosses were to come here and given
command to stop threats, then, I would have giving up at that
point. However, really at that time."
Suzuki immediately takes up the idea.
"Allow me to attempt to get somebody here. However honestly
any official I viewed would initially have as reactivated. With
the new constitution Japan just has a tiny armed force, and only
for motivations behind self-preservation."
Suzuki begins doing totals.
"I might be returning back to Tokyo in few days time. Then
suppose an additional ten days to orchestrate everything. I could
be here again in three weeks."
Onoda reflects rapidly. "That sounds conceivable."
Suzuki hustles: "What do you share with the accompanying
idea? We meet here again in precisely this spot. I'll bring one of
your previous bosses. No Filipino soldiers. No other person. Just
him and me."
Onoda's tone waxes formal. "I acknowledge. In any case,
assuming you attempt to deceive me, I will start shooting
without advance notice on you and any other person with you."

No handshake, simply a brief bow. The men don't contact.
Suzuki feels encouraged. "Would you see any problems in the
event that I snapped a photo of you?"
"No," says Onoda. "Provided that we're both in it together."
Suzuki recovers his camera. Since he doesn't have a stand, he
puts it on his backpack. He hops back to Onoda, who is hunching
down on the ground six feet away.

"There'll be a glimmer any second. You presumably have no clue
about what a sensation the image will be from one side of the
planet to the other."
"Hold my rifle," says Onoda. "That can be confirmation that I
trust you."
The two men are washed in the blaze. Onoda grimaces at Suzuki.
"In any case, part of the way. Part of the way."

Lubang Airfield

December 1944

The landing strip is little, with broke, cleaned out black-top that hasn't been fixed in years. There are a couple of single-story structures behind the scenes, rusted tin rooftops, all in shifting phases of disregard. On the opposite side of the strip is the vast ocean, with the little island of Cabra toward the North, scarcely apparent in the murkiness. A Japanese troop carrier is at anchor simply seaward. Little, ungainly landing create are shipping Japanese soldiers out to it. A legion of tired Japanese warriors has walked up in line. Their regalia have not had the wilderness completely cleaned out of them, a couple of the men are wearing rain boots they probably got from local people. As they walk toward the arrival make, they pass the destruction of two military aircraft that has been cleaned up the runway.

Major Taniguchi and Onoda, thirty years his lesser, in the shade of a vacant storage. Onoda, standing ready, is getting orders from his boss. The Major is formal.
"Lieutenant Onoda, I have orders for you from base camp."
Onoda stands somewhat more firmly.
"Indeed, sir, Lieutenant Onoda at your order."
"You are the best man who has encountered preparing covertly fighting here, in guerrilla methods."
"Sir. Major."
"These are your orders. When our soldiers have been removed from Lubang, it is your obligation to hold the island until the Imperial Army's return. You are to guard its region by guerrilla strategies, no matter what. You should settle on your own choices. Nobody will provide you arranges. You should be

independent. From this time forward there are no more standards, you make the principles."

Onoda is apathetic. "Indeed, sir. Major."

"There is just a single rule," Taniguchi proceeds. "You are prohibited to kick the bucket by your own hand. In case of your catch by the adversary, you are to give them all the deceptive data you can."

The Major allures Onoda into the nearly cleared storage. All that here looks transitory. No Japanese planes being refitted, simply a messy load of arrangements and military hardware. The two officials approach a wall that actually has a few guides stuck to it; one is of the island of Lubang. The Major focuses to it.

"You have two quick undertakings, at this moment, even before the departure is finished. One: all explosives still on the island are set influenced quite a bit by. With them you are to obliterate this runway. Two: with any leftover hazardous, you are to obliterate the arrival dock at Tilik. These are the two prime passageways to the adversary."

Onoda concentrates on the guide. The island is an oval shape, a few 25 kilometers long. In its focal area it is sloping and congested with wilderness, with practically no streets or settlements. Confronting Tilik, and not a long way from the town of Lubang toward the North, lies the Bay of Manila, nearly eighty kilometers far off. The restricted southwestern tip of the island, across the slopes, is level, yet again with next to no detectable streets. All there is one little town: Looc.

Onoda inquires: "What number of men will I have under my order, sir?"

"We will assemble a troop for you, Onoda," says the Major. "Honestly, there will not be anybody among them who is a specialist in secret fighting. Also, nobody will be familiar with your orders. In this kind of fighting, there is no possibility of decorations."

"I don't battle for awards."

The men don't talk.

"Sir?" asks Onoda.

"Assuming you have questions, ask now. This is your opportunity."

"Will my obligation be restricted to Lubang, or do I have a more extensive circle of tasks? The little distant islands — Cabra, Ambil, Golo?"

"For what reason do you inquire?"

"Major, the island is not that especially tremendous, and it's 66% peddled in the wild. It's very little for a guerrilla war."

"Onoda, you ought to remember that Lubang's essential importance is all the more prominent," answers the Major. "At the point when the Imperial Army returns in win, we will involve it as a take off platform for an extraordinary assault on the Bay of Manila. The foe will have thought every one of its powers there."

Onoda's demeanor stays misty.

The Major needs no chance of misconception. "Your headquarters will be the wilderness. Your mission will be one of steady loss. Clashes, ambushes, flighty assaults. You will resemble a phantom, slippery, a proceeding with bad dream to the foe. Your conflict will be without magnificence."

Lubang

January 1945

Memories, or perhaps dreams, of the following days are hazy, have taken on an unmistakable overflow of energy. Pieces of things, dependent upon change and revamp, difficult to get a handle on and without a plan, similar to a winder of dried leaves that in any case shows where it is going or perhaps where it has come from. Thus, a truck, seized by the Japanese and utilized just of late for the vehicle of earth and timber, slithering along a sloppy street. The landscape is level, it is pouring. They are some place in the northern piece of the island. Wet banana estates on one or the other side, coconut palms farther off. Several water bison remaining next to a cabin roofed with palm fronds, so unmoving like they had been that way for a really long time. Onoda and six men are clustered on the bed of the truck under a piece of material sheeting, wet, weighty, and sore. Close to Onoda in the sparse sanctuary is Corporal Shimada, a youthful trooper in his mid twenties. A few Filipino residents stop the truck, request that they take their debilitated water bison some place, however the Japanese reject.

A weapons dump on the edge of the wilderness, simply a shed thumped together from sheets of layered metal by a modest bunch of men. A strong breeze. Right now the slopes start, thickly covered with steaming backwoods. Japanese fighters leap off the truck and pull open the door, which is only a wooden casing filled in with corroded metal sheeting. In the gloaming there are stores of mortar and big guns shells. An unexpected breeze blast tears the door from the fighter's hand and pummels it against the structure so hard that it falls to pieces, and bits of sheeting take off. One single piece is left holding tight the casing; it is whistling in the hurricane.

Onoda is angry, however aces himself. Or on the other hand is it that this scene has been created in his memory with the advantage of knowing the past? Right close to the weapons are a couple of thumped looking metal barrels. Onoda tests the items in one with a bamboo test. "Corporal Shimada, these barrels contain petroleum. Petroleum and explosives should never be put away together. Who is mindful?"
Shimada shrugs. "No one makes a great deal or cares any longer about those military standards."
Onoda raises his voice, he believes everybody should hear him. "From this point forward, I'm in control. We as a whole hold equivalent obligation. We are the military."
Shimada glances around. "Sir, I get it. A multitude of seven."

Be that as it may, it is Shimada, who experienced childhood with, a homestead answer for the expulsion of the heaviest bombs, which weigh a portion of a ton each.
"Lieutenant," he guarantees Onoda, "back home we once hauled 1,000 hammer bull out of a marsh." Under his guidelines, a tree trunk is quickly changed over into a switch, whose turn is shaped by a few of the petroleum barrels trundled together. A bomb of tremendous type is then raised on the more limited piece of the tree trunk and turned up onto the truck bed. Once showed up at the runway with his heap, Onoda immediately is engaged with a showdown with the leader there, Lieutenant Hayakawa, who is reluctant to let any of his own men assist with emptying the bombs onto the airstrip.
"The pulling out units," he announces, "require the airstrip for the clearing of weighty matériel." Hayakawa additionally believes the airstrip should stay in one piece until such time as the Imperial Air Forces recover control of the skies. However,

Onoda, however dedicated to quiet, has his own, secret, orders to follow.

"This airstrip will be taken by the foe," he says, "except if we extensively obliterate it. If not they will basically utilize it against us. Do you comprehend that the total clearing of Lubang has been requested?"

Hayakawa takes shelter in misleading publicity: "Our brilliant pilots will before long be requiring this landing strip in the future. Our withdrawal is transitory and strategic."

Lubang, Tilik

January 1945

Anxiety. Haziness. The wharf at Tilik broadens approximately seventy meters into the sound. Onoda and his men are in the middle of fixing sticks of explosive and different explosives to the backings, while above Japanese warriors befuddled in the murkiness are attempting to track down departure vessels. A couple of spotlights make wild tracks in the night sky. Officers bounce into fishing boats, which are, nonetheless, uncrewed and restricted. At last, an arrival make gets some of the leaderless Japanese soldiers. The Japanese withdrawal is scattered in the limit.

Onoda provides orders that the wharf props are to be dynamited each ten meters. Corporal Shimada wires up the explosives with electrical wire, however is adequately realistic — measure two times, slice once — to twofold it up with combine wire since he has little to no faith in the power supply. He holds an electric lamp grasped between his teeth. An official ends up seeing what is happening. He moves toward Onoda: "You are dynamiting this dock, is that right?"
"Chief, that is precisely exact thing I'm doing."
"I believe you should stop, and that is a request."
Onoda remains totally quiet. "I have extraordinary orders of my own."
This irritates the official. "Man, can't you observe how our soldiers are using the wharf? Tomorrow first thing there will be a greater amount of them, and we'll be going through this way for something like two additional days. There are units in the inside with which we have lost contact."

Onoda thinks briefly. "My orders permit me some scope. Yet, the foe is coming. When our men have left the island, I will leave on crafted by annihilation."

At first light, Onoda has the truck leave on the border of Tilik. He gathers all that he really wants. Deserted weapons boxes loaded with projectiles, hand explosives, rice sacks with a field kitchen. Close to it an enormous tent, with every one of the sides moved up. There are warriors lying on basic field beds. Just now does Onoda understand this is a field medical clinic. An injured man pulls himself up and requests a few explosives. Large numbers of the men have grave wounds and would prefer to end it all than fall into adversary hands.
"You might not be cleared right? Who is gathering you?" asks Onoda.
"Nobody," answers the injured man.
"Nobody?"
"We have been deserted. Recently there were two clinical orderlies, however they left when dimness fell. They said they needed to proceed to take care of certain setbacks in Tilik, yet we end up realizing there has been no battling in or around Tilik throughout recent weeks." the soldier made a sitting position, despite his serious injury. "I have idea on how to turn off bombs."
Onoda reflects rapidly. "Okay, I'll leave you a portion of our explosives. Is it true that you are as yet ready to toss a hand projectile?"
"Leave the explosives by my bed, and I will simply pull the trigger," the trooper guarantees him.

Starting here, Onoda's recollections are obscured. The main clear thing is that he couldn't obliterate the runway at Lubang. The wide range of various units are uncooperative, no soldiers are supported to him, troops who could never have been his to order, regardless — the radar unit, the ack unit, the ground groups for the planes, the crew liable for the maritime units, who have been left without a CO. Onoda's thought then is to allow the adversary to obliterate the landing strip. Along with a couple of reluctant people from the beginning, he hauls several shot-up military aircraft onto the runway and roughly sets them up so that from the air they could have all the earmarks of being planes good to go to go up.

"Our bosses should have developed such frameworks previously," Onoda says.

Lieutenant Hayakawa finds this type of fight dishonorable. "I will battle for the distinction of our Emperor, and in good battle."

"How would you?" Onoda inquires. In any case, Hayakawa finds such weakness undeserving of an answer. In the long years to come, Onoda will over and over ponder the manner in which animals guard themselves in nature, how they make themselves undetectable like moths assuming the blotches of tree rind, fish whose shading matches the rocks on the riverbed, bugs that look like the green leaves of trees, insects like malicious harpists culling powerful tunes from their strings and in this way make the snare of an adversary species vibrate similarly like a bug had become up to speed in them. Consumed by interest, the sovereign insect moves toward the web, and her destruction. Or on the other hand the snake whose clatter occupies the hare from the human peril drawing closer. The remote ocean fish whose light sign baits more modest fish that in this way permit themselves to be caught. Also, how do such animals safeguard themselves? By pretending to be dead, similar to the insect that lies on its back. By the spines of desert flora and thistle trees or the plumes from creatures like the porcupine, the hedgehog, the barbed fish that simultaneously can expand themselves so much that they are too huge to be gulped. Wellbeing in poison, similarly as with wasps and snakes and stinging brambles; by shocks, as from the electric eel, and by rank discharges, just like with skunks; by a thick cloak of ink from octopi. Confusion, ploy, mimicry — all components that Onoda needs to gain from nature, whether respectable etc. The main models are adequacy in fight and accomplishing one's goal. Rather than a full-front facing assault with pennants waving, he needs to make himself undetectable, become an intangible dream figure, a tricky and dangerous fog, gossip, a report. Through him the wilderness is to turn out to be in excess of a wilderness, a scene with a dangerous glow of unexpected end.

One final time, Onoda and Shimada attract up external the ad libbed field clinic their truck. The circumstance is as sad as could be expected. The injured man to whom Onoda gave the hand projectile to set off the weapons is scarcely cognizant. Quiet looks follow him from the camp beds. Onoda lines the truck up close by the emergency clinic. He and Shimada shoulder weighty backpacks and snatch their rifles. Joined to Onoda's webbing belt is a samurai blade that has been in his family since the seventeenth hundred years. Up to this point, he has figured out how to protect it any place he has been posted. The two troopers show respect for toward their injured companions and quietly soften into the sloping wilderness that here starts.

Lubang, Jungle

End of January 1945

Onoda and Shimada have disguised themselves in a couple of portions of dirtied material, and are hunkering in thick vegetation on a wilderness slant. Night, far off thunder of mounted guns, and dissipated blasts contact them in waves, similar to the ocean moving up a pebbled ocean side. Bundles of tracer fire define boundaries in the dark air. An extraordinary heater is pounding, similar to an incredible creature breathing fire. Onoda cautiously dislodges a wet twig. "Tilik. Similarly as we anticipated. It's the intrusion."

Shimada wonders whether or not to say it, yet from here on out all that is reality, regardless of whether it can in any case change and foster an unmistakable overflow of energy. "We didn't annihilate the wharf."

Onoda is quiet. "I'm loaded up with disgrace. Be that as it may, nothing can change the reality."

Shimada attempts to offer something consoling. "This attack is so enormous, so overpowering, that we should rest assured the Americans would have arrived here at any rate, dock or no wharf, guarded by us or not."

The next day Onoda and Shimada move up to the highest point of the twin pinnacle. The pale line of the sea is way beneath them to one side. Up here, Japanese soldiers have dug a channel, adequate security for twelve or so troops. A couple of people are lying impassively on the ground, loused up, baffled. A tent has been pitched close by, however there is nobody in it. Ammo cartons are littered about, a tore open sack of rice, cooking gear, all with no great explanation.

"Who is in control here?" Onoda inquires.

"We've been just let alone. What's more, presently I'm going," answers a warrior, and he steps up to the plate and climbs out of the channel.

He has an arrangement as well. To travel South, to Looc, at the opposite finish of the island. From up here on the mountain, they had seen a lot of developments out adrift, toward the East, toward Manila. The adversary had made landfall at Tilik with impressive strength, yet all they appeared to be keen on was the northern piece of the island, with the towns of Lubang and Tilik. Onoda, as far as it matters for him, is sure that the whole island will be dominated. Yet, the man sets off, and a couple more move out of the vile channel and follow him. Onoda can fail to address it. The fighters resist him and walk off. The leftover men dig in still lower in their trench, staying away from eye to eye connection with Onoda. How would they believe they will stand up to? he asks the inclined figures. An immense armed force was going to turn up, with cannons, mortars, and assault rifles, also air support from the US Air Forces. One trooper goes to confront Onoda: "Not in this way, sir. The air backing will be coming from our own Imperial Air Forces."

Onoda has seen and adequately heard. He attracts his sword and focuses the course of the wilderness. "Follow me. It's your main opportunity of additional obstruction. Nobody will make due up here, and nobody at the lower part of the island will endure by the same token."

He tunnels into the thickest piece of the wilderness. Aside from Shimada, no other person follows him. Briefly longer, the passes on keep on stirring, then, at that point, the green wall has gobbled them up.

Lubang

February 1945

Time, time and the wilderness. The wilderness doesn't perceive time. They resemble two distanced kin who will not have anything to do with one another, who impart, if by any means, just as scorn. Days follow evenings, however there are no seasons in that capacity, and no more, months with immense measures of downpour and months with somewhat less downpour. There is one unvarying steady: all that in the wilderness is making careful effort to choke all the other things in the fight for daylight. It very well might be completely dark around evening time, however nothing changes the mind-boggling, inflexible current state of the wilderness. Bird sounds and the sharp of crickets, like an extraordinary train had applied its crisis slows down and were screaking wildly along the rails, for a really long time, ceaselessly. Then, at that point, like under the implement of a ghost director, they unexpectedly fall quiet, at the same time; the ensemble wheezes and pauses its breathing. Onoda and Shimada duck at the same time. The birds, as well, are quiet. An admonition? Some coming risk? Nothing blends. Then the strong sharp of the crickets resumes, again at the same time, synchronized to a small part of a second.

Shimada takes a chance with a murmured correspondence. "I know where the rice terminal is."

"On Snake Mountain," risks Onoda.

"No, some way from that point, at Hill 500." Shimada knows the specific spot. "I trust the rice is still there."

Slope 500 is an optimal post, one of the greatest heights on Lubang; not at all like the wide range of various tops on the island, it isn't congested. The jutting protuberance seems to be a bare head standing out, just a little knee-high grass develops here. It bears the cost of a perspective on the whole North and West of the island. Onoda and Shimada spend seemingly forever unmoving in the haven of the woodland periphery. Something mixes there, underneath them, a sound. They stay unbendingly still, with the scarcely conceivable persistence of wild creatures. To a puma in the open, it's completely regular. Furthermore, Onoda is presently a creature, a spotted creature. With his field glasses he clears the wilderness before him, without the least articulation. At the point when he hands them to Shimada, it is in sluggish movement, where a straightforward motion appears to require minutes — require weeks — like they were an outgrowth of his hand that should have been relocated. Or on the other hand is it only seconds, so profoundly and seriously felt that they appeared to happen for quite a long time?

Level fields toward the North of the island, rice, coconut palms, a couple of little villages of five or six hovels each, mounted on poles, roofed with palm leaves. Far off protest of blasts. Up in the North, the beach is covered with murkiness, with an unmistakable layer of hazier cloudiness hanging above it. Shimada spots fire on the landing strip up there. He returns the field glasses. From this point forward, they just impart in murmurs. Onoda appears to be unaffected. "The Americans have besieged the runway," he murmurs, "when they might have involved it for their planes. It's a triumph for us. Our most memorable triumph."

Encouraged, the two troopers leave their concealing spot, Onoda generally on the actual edge of the wilderness, prepared to give covering fire to Shimada, who is carefully out in the open. He arrives at a heap of dried palm fronds and starts pulling them away each in turn. Hidden under them is various metal canisters, all unfilled. All aside from the last, which is loaded with rice. Wooden cases likewise covered up are overflowing with ammo, a few thousand rifle slugs, automatic weapon belts. Cautiously the two officers recuperate their find. Onoda looks at the rice, holds a couple of grains out in the light in the center of his hand. No soggy, no indication of form. The trees around shake tenderly. Onoda's hand shakes, as well, not a real shudder yet a compulsory trembling, similar to the skin of a pony attempting to safeguard itself against flies. The couple of grains of rice take off, obviously independently. Then, at that point, a tension wave, and a brief instant later the thunder roll of a colossal far off blast. Onoda without a moment's delay comprehends that this probably been the field emergency clinic. The injured men have exploded themselves, no inquiry. Onoda and Shimada bow officially toward the blast, and stand firm on the footing for quite a while. From that point onward, Onoda and Shimada are coming, off into the many years that lie in front of them. Frequently strolling in reverse so their follows are going off course. Along these lines, they experience two additional Japanese troopers who are lying on the ground, rifles positioned. Immediately Onoda and Shimada seek shelter. One of different troopers, expecting fortifications, jumps up. Quickly he is struck by a volley of fire from the opposite side, and probably killed. The subsequent man messes up the same way and sets out on a crisscross run toward Onoda, who starts shooting toward the concealed foe. By some marvel, the man isn't hit. He drops down among Onoda and Shimada in a little empty on the wilderness' edge. Hints of American voices, clearly withdrawing; the wilderness is excessively risky for them. Onoda holds the fresh introduction back from keeping an eye on his companion. A dead man would just be a hindrance to them.

"Who are you?" asks Onoda.

"Confidential Kozuka."

"Who is the man around there?"

"Confidential Muranaka."

"I'm in order here. On the off chance that the Private is as yet alive, I will get him. Cover me." Onoda takes off his backpack and takes out his sword. Like a samurai in a dangerous wrath, he jumps up and races in a custom assault directly toward the foe, who has cleared his snare. Onoda finds the man lying facedown and turns him over. He is dead.

Night. The men, three of them currently, tend a little fire in an empty among thick foliage. Onoda is distracted. "My blade assault was show. I was playing a samurai in a film. An indefensible pass. The conflict is different now, brave signals have no spot. Our undertakings are to stay undetectable, to hoodwink the foe, to be prepared to do apparently offensive things while being careful in our souls the champion's honor." The men have heated up some rice. They eat peacefully. Then Kozuka lets them know he was an individual from the landing strip ground team. Initially there were seven of them. Four more had gone along with them, just to leave again hours after the fact. They had missed the mark on administrator. "How could the trap be the case?" asks Onoda. Kozuka answers that nobody anticipated that the adversary should come nearer from the South. These high priority come from the ocean side of the island. They had a good sense of reassurance, when unexpectedly they had experienced harsh criticism. Just he and Muranaka had figured out how to move away to higher elevation.

"Who were the men killed? Do I know them?" Onoda inquires.

"Ito, Suehiro, Kasai."

"I knew Kasai," says Onoda.

"Kasai was hit in the head. And afterward Osaki and quite recently Muranaka. We went to class together."

Quiet comes over the men. Kozuka is eager to the point that he scratches the vacant rice pot with his fingers. He had last eaten three days prior, before the runway was taken. "What occurred there?" Onoda asks; he had seen fire.

"American military aircraft made an unopposed assault and shot up the spurious planes on the runway," Kozuka reports.
"I put them there," says Onoda.
"So it was you who deluded the adversary."
Onoda doesn't grin. " "The US destroyed what would have been their next jumping-off point by their hands."
Kozuka is hesitant to continue. "They didn't actually obliterate the runway."
"Your meaning could be a little clearer."
"They dropped no bombs. They didn't hole the surface."
"Really?"
"They just used their machine guns to strafe the dummy planes, setting them on fire. The airstrip is for the most part flawless."
Onoda is quiet. Sooner or later he looks at his new companion in the eye. "I have lost my honor. First the dock at Tilik, which is as yet unblemished, and presently the airstrip. From here onward our watchword should be: assault the foe, incur misfortunes for him, and pull out."
Kozuka joins their small troop, which is presently up to three men.
"We as a whole in Lubang realize that you would have subverted the wharf at Tilik however for a few senior officials. We can in any case complete many assignments. The three of us will actually want to go against the adversary in numerous ways. They won't ever track down us. The American watches make an excess of clamor, and they are careful about the wilderness."

Around evening time, when the men have set up a tent in the thick underbrush, and Kozuka is wheezing erratically, Onoda unobtrusively goes up to Shimada, who is on watch. They momentarily banter whether to keep the fresh introduction with them. They recognize that he is solid, furthermore, he has no unit any longer, and no goal. Onoda would like him still to demonstrate his value. The next morning, he has vanished.

However, when Onoda asks Shimada discreetly where he may be, the two of them hear Kozuka's voice. He is close by, on watch, thus thickly disguised with leaves that he is by all accounts part of the wilderness. Farther, he has tracked down a wellspring of new water a couple of moments underneath their situation. One container full, covered with a banana leaf, he has proactively bubbled. At the point when the individuals from the post were put to flight, they practically completely experienced the runs drinking out of streams. In every one of the years to come, the battle to stay solid will be fundamental. With the exception of when they find pools of water on enormous leaves, they will continuously heat up their water.

Lubang, Close to Tilik

Late February 1945

This is where the temporary field emergency clinic once stood. Onoda and his two confidants warily investigate the territory. Tilik town, involved by the intruders, isn't far. Nothing remains to show what once, in the relatively recent past, was here. High up in a tree Onoda makes the strange disclosure of a boot, got on its bands in a limb. It's a Japanese armed force boot. Leaving their cover, the fighters approach and see something that makes their blood freeze. Before them is an empty cavity, with a little water at the lower part of it. Essentially nothing remains, no tent, no carcass, not even any body parts, everything has apparently vanished, dematerialized in the intensity. The three men quietly salute.

Onoda realizes that they can endure provided that they intermittently tear out of the dark to arrangement themselves. The wilderness will give them nothing. The procurement of food makes them defenseless. Their pushes should be speedy and exact, and come after comprehensive perception of the scene. In the plain they are apparent to the adversary; just around evening time or during heavy downpour are they — potentially — safe. At sunset they lurk into a woods of palms and are shocked when a young lady strolls by with her doggy. She was just singing melodies to herself and didn't see them. The pup stops to bark toward Onoda, however when the young lady rushes on under the heightening precipitation, it follows.

They get coconuts that are lying dissipated on the ground, still in their bold green shells. Around evening time in their shelter, the men attempt to break the shells. Kozuka attempts with his blade,

Onoda wounds his with his knife. Tragically, this piece of their schooling was ignored in military foundation. Shimada tracks down the arrangement. He puts the coconut down on a level stone and strikes the tip of it with a major stone. The entire of the thick strip swells outward. Then with a blade the thick snare of green filaments effectively allows itself to be disengaged from the nut.

"Obviously," says Onoda. "The homestead kid takes care of the issue."

"Not in any way shape or form," counters Shimada, "that was simply knowledge. On our homestead we didn't develop coconuts."

It is maybe their most memorable snapshot of levity. The heaviness of the next many years will totally squash such minutes, including this one. A sound. The men freeze. Kozuka contacts his ear, movements with his head, down there some place. Carefully, Onoda takes up his rifle. Is it an individual drawing closer? Presently nothing blends, simply trickles of water from the trees.

"Cover me," Onoda shows to Kozuka; he scarcely moves his lips, it is an imperceptible murmur. He hops up, charges off. A concise battle in the knot beneath the camp. A holler, a Japanese voice.

"I'm one of you. A companion. Japanese. Who are you?"

"To start with, who are you?" counters Onoda.

"Akatsu. Confidential Akatsu. I was essential for the enduring airstrip post under Corporal Fujitsu."

"For what reason would you confirm or deny that you are with them now?"

"Furthermore, where is your weapon?" asks Shimada. "We can utilize men who are outfitted."

Akatsu apologizes. "The fact that I left my rifle makes us in such a rush."

"An officer cannot be without his rifle because there's nothing like that It ought to resemble a piece of him," Onoda reprimands him. "I have an extra gun in my backpack, yet very little ammo." Shimada appears to have greater antagonism toward the newbie. "How about you return to your unit?"

"My unit was pummeled, the couple of men remaining are at this point not on the island." He eliminates his scenes. "I can't find in obscurity. I'm for all intents and purposes night-blind." He cleans them on his neck material. "Also, when it downpours, they haze up. If it's not too much trouble, let me go with you."

"You can remain until tomorrow first thing. We'll choose how to manage you then, at that point," Onoda orders.

Throughout the long night, Onoda and his two men get familiar with Akatsu's story. His unit was nearly without food, and what little they had before long vanished. Akatsu was persuaded that a portion of the men were stealing. They attempted to avoid doubt onto him, attempted to dispose of him since he understood what was happening. He was two times sent away, yet each time got back to the unit since he could never have made due all alone. Then, at that point, an enormous piece of the unit walked straightforwardly into a camp of Filipino soldiers who quickly started shooting at them. Five passed on, others gave up, the leftover, more than forty in number, figured out how to arrive at an arrival make. Him and two others, who were comparably debased by the unit, stayed safe, yet the two others deserted him the next night. The foe attempted to prompt the dispersed survivors to give up; over an amplifier they named a spot, in Japanese, where Japanese troopers could securely give up, yet Akatsu couldn't track down it.

"Confidential Akatsu," Onoda asks him, "let me know what direction is North."

Akatsu glances around cluelessly. No, he can't really understand.

"Confidential Kozuka, what direction is North," Onoda inquires. Kozuka signals superficially with his head. Shimada gestures in affirmation. Onoda removes his gun from his backpack and hands it to Akatsu. "Do you have any idea about how to utilize one of these?"
Akatsu says timidly, "Yes. Not actually. Ambiguously."
"Then, at that point, I'll need to show you," says Onoda, and with that Akatsu has been temporarily enlisted into their unit.

Following a confined night in the tent that is excessively little for four men, Onoda chooses to scrap it through and through; a lot of stuff, likewise it's something simple for the foe to detect. From here onward they never stop anyplace for over a day at an at once, on Onoda is in ceaseless development, in some cases even around evening time. Akatsu experiences difficulty keeping up, he frequently drops off the speed. He is sorry to Onoda.
"Lieutenant, I have not in anyway been in a wilderness, however, I give a valiant effort
"Not a solitary one of us has at any point been in a wilderness," Onoda brings up, however he has some compassion for Akatsu, whose feet are draining in light of the fact that his boots don't fit as expected.
"This resembles a green damnation," says Akatsu unfortunately.
"No, it's simply a woodland in the jungles," says Onoda.

Lubang, Looc Overlook

October 1945

Right now, the wilderness falls steeply away. The Looc plain stretches out from here toward the South coast. Coconut palms, rice paddies, one of them somewhat confined from the others, not piece of a similar water system framework, the field of the one white-hidden lady. Cloudiness. The little town of Looc is faintly apparent on the wide sandy sound. There is no apparent street correspondence toward the North of the island, no boats in the cove, it's like the Americans had never landed. Far somewhere far off, the islands of Golo and Ambil toward the East, the two of them militarily futile, similarly as Lubang was and presently is again pointless. It's just in hypothetical intrusion designs that Lubang has an essential capability as an island, with the additional trouble that it is inhabited by phantoms. Onoda and his men watch out.

A breath of wind blows through the wilderness, slivers of insects' networks are blown away, and with them the months, with nothing to hold them, no shudder twigs, no trickling precipitation. Nothing occurred, only a couple of breaths.

Months after the fact: a similar spot, a similar little troop, again quietly reviewing the plain underneath. Onoda and his three men have transformed: they are better masked; their hair is tangled; their clothing, hardware, and boots have all been spread with mud for motivations behind disguise. They have become one with the wilderness. Onoda orders Akatsu to get water from a little stream underneath their situation, and keeping in mind that he is too far to hear, the other three examine how is to be managed him. Shimada is unsure, Kozuka is agreeable to dumping him. In their innermost being, they generally needed to be freed of him, he was a weight on them, them four were more fragile than they would be in the event that they were just three. Be that as it may, Onoda chooses in any case, regardless of whether Akatsu is a weight, he is as yet a warrior like most of them.

"Are you going to neglect me if I become sick somehow?" he asks Kozuka. "Lieutenant!" Kozuka hurries to guarantee him he would take him on his back and convey him. The far off clamor of a little plane drawing nearer from the heading of Looc makes the men freeze, and they soften once more into the hedge. Onoda tracks it with his field glasses. When it arrives at the steeply rising wilderness close to them, it appears to drop something that scatters on the breeze, something like a lot of confetti.

It requires Akatsu a long investment to get back from his errand, so the other three considering could have come upon him. Did he lose as he would prefer? Did the plane caution him? As sunsets, there is a stir in the underbrush, not before time. Akatsu recognizes himself before they can begin taking shots at him. He is sorry for having spilled a portion of the water, yet he needed to seek shelter out of nowhere due to the plane. He had seen that what the plane had dropped should be handouts. He had spotted one not a long way from where he was, made up for lost time in the highest point of a tree. With trouble he had moved up it, got the handout, and been set upon by fire subterranean insects. What's more, for a reality his hands are enlarged and the lymph organs in his armpits are up. He felt hot, yet he had figured out how to find his direction back since he recollected that Looc was toward the South, thus he realized what direction was North, and their ongoing safe-house. With difficult fingers he attempts to haul the collapsed handout out of his front pocket, however they are enlarged to the point that Onoda needs to help him. The paper is modest, the text on it is imprinted in Japanese.

The men pore over the text, which is endorsed by General Yamashita, Fourteenth Army, and dated August 15. The conflict is finished, it says.

"In any case, it's October presently," says Kozuka tastelessly, "and it doesn't say who won." And there's something else too, something that will arrange contemplated questions into a predictable end: there are botches in a portion of the Japanese characters. Onoda is quick to take note. All Japanese troopers are to rise out of the wilderness into "open view" and give their weapons over to the Philippine Army. It seems like a terrible interpretation, from somebody who doesn't actually know the Japanese language. What's more, a further error: "You will be 'conveyanced' home." The main conceivable end is that this pamphlet is a fraud, probably crafted by American specialists. A misprint is not feasible, regardless of whether the Japanese person for return, convey looks like the one for transport. They should wonder why the hostile aviation based armed forces is still after them, and why Filipino soldiers were as of late ambushing and killing Japanese soldiers, as the case of Akatsu demonstrated. In any case, Akatsu stays dubious; consider the possibility that the conflict truly is finished. Yet, Onoda is unflinchingly persuaded that this is only a stunt to bait them out of their wilderness speed.

"Yet, imagine a scenario where the conflict truly is lost?" Akatsu speaks up once more. Yet, that just supports Onoda in his sureness that the Japanese powers will one day wonderfully return and retake Lubang. The island was of incredible vital significance, and from here the Japanese powers would crowd out to retake the entire Pacific. Their orders were orders.

There is a long interruption. Shimada troubles a creeper. Kozuka shaves away at a piece of wood. Onoda glances around. "Does anybody here need to give up?" He fixes on Akatsu. "Secret

Akatsu, you are permitted to go accepting you really want; I'm not compelling you to do anything."
What was the others' take? Akatsu needs to be aware.
"Lieutenant, assuming you continue battling, I will remain with you."
"What's more, you, Private Kozuka?"
"Remain."
Onoda takes a gander at Akatsu once more. "All things considered, Private?"
"I'm remaining as well. Where might I go without anyone else?"
A further pamphlet affirms Onoda's at this point practically strict faith in the ineptitude of the foe and his imitations. It specifies the prefecture of Wakayama, Onoda's home, like to make him achy to visit the family. In any case, the securing proof is the name of his regiment. This name was changed simply a question of weeks before the Japanese key withdrawal, why Onoda can't say, however the new name sounded bolder, and more successful: "The Cradle of Storms. We will ignore the foe like a storm and blow him away."

Right now, it just so happens, another peculiarity starts, a kind of consistent, subtle friendship, a characteristic dream kin furnished with all the unquestioning sureness of dreams: an unclear season of noctambulism, despite the fact that things carry on as in the past, prompt, substantial, repulsive, irrefutable in their imperiousness — the wilderness; the marsh; the bloodsuckers; the mosquitoes; the shouts of the birds; thirst; the rough, tingling skin. The fantasy has its own time span, it races forward and back, it sticks, halts abruptly, pauses its breathing, gets out ahead like a terrified deer. A night bird screams and a year passes. A fat drop of water on the waxy leaf of a banana plant shimmers momentarily in the sun and one more year is no more. A segment of a great many subterranean insects shows up for the time being and walks through the trees with no start or end; the section walks for a really long time and afterward one day is bafflingly and unexpectedly gone, and that is one more year. Then one single watch under wilting foe fire, and the night appears to continue for all eternity. Just the unexpected flares of tracer shots while day won't break, despite the fact that you check the time and see the hands moving and see the entire of the night sky wheeling around the North Star. Day will not and will not and won't show up. Time outside their lives appears to have the nature of a fit, despite the fact that it can't shake the imperturbable universe. Onoda's conflict is of no importance for the universe, for history, for the course of the conflict. Onoda's conflict is shaped from the association of a nonexistent nothing and a fantasy, yet Onoda's conflict, sired by nothing, is by and by overpowering, an occasion blackmailed from forever.

Lubang, Jungle, Snake Mountain

December 1945

The men have fanned out their plunder on a piece of burlap,
everything is significant for their endurance. A liberating
sensation in the temporary camping area. Evening obscures over
the wilderness. Their matches, tragically, have gotten clammy.
Shimada tells the others they are presently not usable. Regardless
of whether they were dried out in the sun, they would never
again strike. How could he know something like this? ponders
Kozuka. He experienced childhood with a ranch, Shimada
reminds him.

At dusk, Onoda characterizes the new resting plans. He slithers
off under a shrubbery, the territory is slanting.
"You ought to find a put that is on a slant. Assuming that the foe
draws near, you will see him without getting up. Keep your rifles
close by consistently. Cover yourselves with a piece of disguised
burlap, and your legs put on a backpack. Like that, you won't
slide downhill in your rest. The backpack is to be kept pressed
and prepared. You should be ready to evaporate in no time.
Waste and dung are to be covered on the double, and
painstakingly covered over with leaves and twigs. Nobody is
ever to see minimal hint of where we made camp. Nobody is to
know where we went through the evening, or by what course we
walked." The men don't say anything, they have perceived. And
afterward Onoda makes sense of how he sees their separate jobs.
"I'm not your commandant. You have not been designated to me
by High Command. I'm your chief."

The next morning, the men set about fixing their garments and
hardware. Kozuka, who has dismantled his rifle, comments that

all pieces of it are covered with a fine layer of rust, the wilderness sodden has gotten in all over. Onoda cautiously draws his sword from its sheath, it, as well, gives indications of rust. There are coconuts all over, yet how would you make palm oil? Nobody knows, not even the ranch kid Shimada. An endeavor to smash some white coconut tissue between two rocks wastes time. Then Kozuka recalls a cook who once worked in Europe, in an Italian eatery. He later lived close to his family's shoemaker shop. Kozuka recollects the cook discussing the mark on Italian olive oil: additional virgin. "What did that have to do with coconuts?" Onoda inquires. Kozuka recalls his discussion with the cook: additional virgin oil was costly in light of the fact that the olives were not warmed. So olive oil can in any case be made utilizing heat. It will require weeks more before the troopers prevail with regards to refining palm oil. They start by demanding a huge cooking pot from a town; then they crush the tissue of coconuts and blend it in with water and intensity the harsh squash over a strangely enormous fire. Since the smoke would be effectively noticeable, they hang tight for a day; the wilderness is cloudy. Initial, a thick foam is encouraged, and after that dies down, a layer of oil, which can be painstakingly gathered up. Thereupon, Onoda can keep his gun and his family treasure in great shape for very nearly thirty years. Shots, which are additionally transitory, are kept upstanding in oil, fixed in taken bricklayer jolts, and covered in the wilderness, all things considered 2,000 400 rifle adjusts, a few hundred gun adjusts, and a few hundred huge type adjusts for automatic rifles. Onoda demands that they not be discarded, after a short time they will demonstrate their utilization in making fires. Since how would you get a fire going without an inventory of dry matches? They make numerous vain endeavors to turn a stick in their grasp over a piece of dry wood to make sufficient grinding to make a fire. This was the technique Onoda learned in his course for expert fighting, however here everything is excessively sodden for it to work.

A couple of months after the fact, from furtively noticing a couple of Filipino woodcutters through their field glasses, do they get the technique the islanders use to make fire out of entryways. They split an arm-thick piece of bamboo in two longwise, and make one of them quick to the ground, similar to a rail. The other one is painstakingly cut open, somewhat cut that scarcely infiltrates the bamboo. Two men kneeling down, confronting one another, take the free 50% of bamboo, with the entry point, and rub it rapidly this way and that over the rail. The strain and rubbing produce such an excess of intensity that a little heap of bamboo shavings at last starts to gleam. At the point when there is downpour or the air is especially sodden, Onoda likes to add a little powder from the automatic weapon ammo, which in any case would have had no utilization. After brief, rough scouring, a little fire shoots out.

Over one retreat, they lose Akatsu, who indeed has fallen behind. Kozuka, conveyed as an inquiry party, can't track down him. A heavy downpour starts to fall. The feet of the men, who have looked for cover under a huge tree, are canvassed in mud, mosquitoes, and bloodsuckers. Indeed, even huge leaves, held over their heads, can't keep the downpour from getting all over. The tremendous rattle of water charges all that to quietness, man and nature the same.

Lubang, Hill 500 Summit

End of 1945

Since Akatsu is as yet pursued two days, Onoda, Shimada, and Kozuka rebury the load of weapons in another spot so that, if Akatsu has fallen into foe hands, he can't deceive the concealing spot. The wilderness around the uncovered handle of 500 is more appropriate at any rate in light of the fact that from that point you can take in the treeless culmination. Just with a huge mathematical benefit would the foe risk coming up here. Yet again onoda oils his blade, enveloping handle and sheath by rattan, and bringing down it in an upward direction into an empty tree. He cautiously seals up the spot with earth and greenery.

Akatsu turns up out of the blue on the center of the wilderness way that paves the way to the culmination. He is boundlessly feeling better to have found his unit once more, regardless of whether he leave unmistakable tracks on the way. He says he lost contact when a tie on his backpack tore. He shows them how he has attempted to fix it with a liana. He had then become lost, and strolled nearly to the extent that Tilik prior to understanding his misstep. There was no one there on Snake, and he had recently meandered around haphazardly. In an additional five years, in mid 1950, Akatsu will leave the unit once and for all, and give up to Filipino soldiers.

From away somewhere far off, they hear the patter of gunfire, and mortar blasts. Indeed, the foe has tracked down Akatsu's path, however Onoda keeps a reasonable head. Mortars are something you ought to possibly utilize when you know the foe's precise position; this here is only the creation of commotion, an indication of dread, something to demonstrate to the neighborhood people that the Japanese guerrillas are courageously being pursued. More serious peril would come from quiet. Lubang is little to such an extent that it is feasible to lay a few snares immediately, entire trap of them even. In the thirty years, only under, of his singular conflict, Onoda will endure one hundred eleven ambushes.

90 days after Akatsu's acquiescence, Onoda and his now two men look on as a truck weighed down with incredible wooden boxes is driven up Six Hundred Mountain, which bears the cost of a perspective on the town of Gontin and the Bay of One House Village. The containers end up being amplifiers. Sections of a voice are exploded to them, hard to make out, yet at the same conspicuously Japanese. Subsequent to listening hard, the men concur that it is Akatsu's voice, guaranteeing them that Akatsu was being treated with deference. However, certainly feasible that a voice imitator was utilized. Onoda accepts Akatsu has been tormented, to make him talk. The voice rehashes, it is obviously a tape, guaranteeing them that the Filipinos would let Akatsu return home, yet Onoda turns out to be increasingly more sure that this is every one of the a foe stratagem to inspire him to surrender. As smoke is blown away on the breeze, so the breeze scatters the voice. Also, it before long becomes clear that the mission is to be continued. Movement in the air and maritime moves highlight the kickoff of another front some place toward the West. Yet, that was at that point the conflict later, for America.

Rice Paddy, Northern Plain of Lubang

Mid 1946

The rice fields here stretch nearly to the edge of the wilderness. Several water bison are floundering in a lake, lowered up to their backs in the sloppy water. Occasionally one waggles its ears. On a field track is another, lone, bison saddled to a two-wheeled truck, his head so low he seems to be sleeping on his feet. A little gathering of rice ranchers, wearing wide-overflowed straw caps, shirts, and undergarments, is twisting around and working endlessly, calf somewhere down in water. Each time one maneuvers his feet there's a smacking sound, generally complete quietness; they take care of their responsibilities peacefully, establishing the new rice shoots in the mud under the water. Other than a feeling of the day reaching a conclusion, there is no sign of the time. It's like it were taboo — there's not so much as a genuine feeling of present on the grounds that each performed activity is now previously, and each resulting one is future. All here are outside history, which in its withdrawnness won't permit present. The rice is planted, collected, planted once more. Realms fall into rot. Quietness. In the quietness of endless time periods, shots ring out. The laborers escape.

From the wilderness edge Onoda and his two men come charging out of the shadows. Every one understands what he should do. Onoda discharge another shot toward the escaping laborers, Kozuka kills the bison tackled to the truck with an authoritative shot in the head, Shimada with energetic developments begins cutting off the rear legs of the dead monster. They are old hands at this, having done it all often previously. Kozuka cuts long pieces of meat along the spine. There is no assault to be dreaded from the far off town. The other water bison, remaining in the soil, exhausted, show no inclination. Then, weighed down with their weighty abundance, the men pull out. Notwithstanding the portions of meat over his backpack, Onoda is conveying a bison leg in his arms, like carrying an injured ally to somewhere safe and secure. The men realize that in the oncoming obscurity not so much as a very much furnished troop of the foe will try to follow them into the wilderness.

"Mist is our dearest companion," notices Onoda, while proceeding to rake the smoking fire with a stick. The entire wilderness is fogbound, a light sprinkle is falling. Just in conditions like this could the men at any point keep the smoke and consequently their whereabouts mysterious. Shimada continues to place bits of bark into the flares, which ease up the shade of the smoke to match the white haze. On a jury-manipulated spit, portions of meat are hanging to smoke. In the sweltering, soggy environment untreated meat ruins inside two days. There is a period for meat, a period for coconuts, a period for rice. Onoda assaults the rice harvests — typically taking two sacks of rice, no more. He would rather not have such a large number of fighters dispatched to find him, he might want to keep the island liberated from Philippine powers, if conceivable. On its possible return, the Imperial Army shouldn't need to experience an excessive number of adversary troops. At the point when on one event he infiltrates the focal point of Tilik, there is an immediate trade of fire. There are injured on the Filipino side, and Shimada is hit in the leg, which will irritate him from here onward, indefinitely. At bottlenecks where Onoda can be depended on to go through frequently, there are rehashed ambushes, with brief firefights. Onoda's mindfulness is the wariness of a wild creature. The lofty congested inclines are moderately protected, yet there is presently not one watering put on Lubang that isn't without some gamble. However, there are likewise minutes when Onoda will unexpectedly come blasting out of the brush, and discharge a shot over the tops of the scared local people, simply to show them that he is still there, actually possessing the island of Lubang. He has turned into a legend. For local people he is the soul of the wilderness, just to be discussed in murmurs. For the Philippine Army, which appears to be unequipped for getting him, he is a long-lasting indication of their insufficiency, however simultaneously the soldiers discuss him with the level of love one could have for a mascot. Two officers who deliberately point their firearms way over his head during a conflict are focused. In any case, there are dead among the Philippine powers too, and among the locals. Onoda never talked about it exhaustively, nor are there any dependable figures from the Philippine specialists. Furthermore, in Japan, in the mean time, the papers keep his single conflict ceaselessly before the consideration of their readership, underscoring the fantasy of the courageous lone trooper, simultaneously keeping alive a difficult sign of Japan's loss in the World War.

Lubang

Stormy Season, 1954

Consistently, Onoda and his two men are progressing. Never do they leave minimal hint of themselves. Just in the three months of the stormy season do they have any feeling that everything is good. Troops will scarcely be dispatched during the storm's end times, and for the span of that period, Onoda fabricates a strong haven of saplings with a raised floor. The design is constantly set up some place in the thickest and steepest piece of the wilderness, and the top of woven palm fronds is rarely shut, so the part confronting the valley is left half open, leaving a perspective on conceivable infringing foes.

A seepage ditch safeguards the cottage from flooding from a higher place, and there is an external latrine concealed from the primary structure. Supplies of rice, green cooking bananas, and smoked meat are kept secure in an extraordinary specialty. This period is especially valued by them three as a period of relative serenity. They fix their gear, rest undisturbed, and the days go by without strain. Just a single time, after years like this, does the stormy season hold off for a very long time or more, and an unfriendly power comes perilously near their concealing spot without finding it. Then, at that point, the downpour recommences and happens for a really long time longer than expected. In the vulnerability of the hours and days, schedules make a slight feeling of safety. The men possibly at any point have conflicts when they feel compromised. Onoda brilliantly never really forestalls these, and their common fury at last blows over.

The stormy season is likewise the ideal opportunity for narrating. Kozuka, obviously, shuts up, his associates advance practically nothing about him, his family, their little shoemaking business, his young spouse who was pregnant when his call-up came. He is perpetually contemplating whether the child is a kid or young lady, and it's beyond what he can do to comprehend that he currently has a ten-year-old of some portrayal. Shimada is more open, he gets a kick out of the chance to chuckle, discusses his home on the ranch and about devices and machines. In any case, both are unquenchable with regards to Onoda and his accounts of his family and his young life. Indeed, even after years spent together, these accounts are limitless due to the manner in which Onoda continues to coincidentally find subtleties he has never referenced. Every one of his friends know about him is that, following his more established sibling to China, he made a lot of cash as an exceptionally young fellow in a general store in Hankow, however it is solely after twenty years that he incorporates the reality — like it were something special to be mortally embarrassed about — that at nineteen years old he was the proprietor of a Studebaker, a make of American vehicle. The youthful Onoda was the primary individual in China to drive a Studebaker.

Shimada's interest is aroused. "Did the young ladies like the vehicle?"

Onoda mulls over everything. "They enjoyed the vehicle better than they loved me." But then, at that point, he adds discreetly that one of the young ladies probably preferred him a considerable amount, such an excess of as a matter of fact that when he took up with another person, she attempted to commit suicide. He had managed ladies and their feelings; according to the perspective of today, his way of behaving was deceitful. How had he then turned into the faithful trooper who all of a sudden, night and day, downpour and sparkle, enduring an onslaught and while being pursued, stood steadfastly to his obligation? Kozuka inquires. Onoda requirements to consider it. It had presumably started with his re-visitation of Japan, and especially when he became intrigued by combative techniques. The defining moment probably accompanied his preparation in kendo, or stick battling. With that, he had come to grasp something of the Japanese soul, and his eyes were at last completely opened when he enlisted in the military. In any case, kendo had shown him that all types of actual battle can be diminished to a quintessence, two men battling with two sticks.

Over and over, the men arrive at this place in their discussions. What ought to war resemble? How is it that it could be improved? In their act of it, with no response to armed force, cannons, naval force, or aircraft planes? However at that point shouldn't something be said about their own guns, the standard-issue armed force rifles they use? From his investigation of hit and run combat, Onoda realizes there was a period once when guns, however currently in far reaching use, were surrendered practically for the time being. It is his #1 subject, interminably captivating to him. Right off the bat in the seventeenth 100 years, with next to no proper choice having been made, the samurai had surrendered their guns. From that time on, all battle was one man to another, with swords or spears, infrequently quits. What denoted the start of this was an extraordinary fight in 1603 in which just 26 warriors actually utilized guns. Shimada objects that guns were utilized all things considered, however Onoda brings up that in an extraordinary fight a decade past, nearly hundred and 80,000 men battled on one side; there was recorded confirmation of this. Around 33% of this military had conveyed guns, making about 60,000 men. Nobody could say with similar accuracy what the figures for the opposite side were, yet any reasonable person would have agreed that a hundred thousand guns were utilized, in addition to gun and falconets. Subsequently, a simple 26 black powder guns 10 years after the fact was near the total shortfall of guns. What had happened then, at that point, Shimada needs to be aware. They got back in the saddle, says Onoda. How long individuals got by without them was unsure. Before long they had returned into utilization. "In some cases," says Onoda, "it feels to me that there is something about these weapons that removes them from human control. Do they have a unique kind of energy, when they're formulated? What's more, doesn't war appear to have an unmistakable overflow of energy as well? Does war long for war?" And then, at that point, after quite a while considering such contemplations, Onoda says something he seldom says, like the thought were a piece of metal brought to white intensity in fire: "Is this possible that i have dreams about this conflict? Might it at any point be that I'm injured in some clinic and will at long last emerged from a trance like state years after the fact, and somebody will let me know it was each of the a fantasy? Is the wilderness, the downpour — everything here — a fantasy? Is Lubang only a dream that exists just on old sailors' diagrams, alongside ocean beasts and people with the heads of mythical serpents and canines?"

Thus the days go by. The downpour beats on their asylum. Water descends the mountain gulping leaves and soil and removed twigs with it. At the point when the downpour eases up, the men check their ammo that has been put away upstanding in oil-filled bricklayer jolts that were expected for canning foods grown from the ground jam; they work on their boots and their garbs, which are scarcely a memory of regalia. The men cook and eat and endlessly rest and eat and cook all through the undefined dark long stretches of water spilling from the mists and hazes bubbling up in nature's brilliant detachment. Consistently, Onoda produces his family blade from its concealing spot, and cautiously cleans and oils it. Regardless of whether he was living in fever dreams, the sword remains his most tangible reference point for something that can't be designed; an anchor dropped in a far off the real world.

However at that point reality resumes influence. Kozuka is debilitated, there is blood in his pee, and Shimada mixes him a tea produced using wilderness plants. His condition stays unaffected. Kozuka unexpectedly detests everything, the wilderness, the downpour, the conflict, the tea, which he continues drinking for good measure. Ammo is by all accounts genuine, as well, not the real shots themselves but rather their numbers, despite the fact that numbers are not obvious. At the point when he cleans the projectiles and moves them on into a new palm oil shower, Onoda holds an enumeration. He utilizes little sticks that he spreads out on the ground and moves as per his very own arrangement creation, a kind of confidential math device, which likewise carries out responsibility as a schedule. There are 2,000 600 rifle shots left; they have a typical yearly utilization of forty. Be that as it may, in spite of all his wariness, he has seen a few indications of oxidation, and, of late, a few shots have would not shoot. In principle, the shots should be really great for an additional sixty years of fighting, yet Onoda underscores economy in their utilization. Imagine a scenario where the enemy were to jump start an unexpected hard and fast assault. Imagine a scenario in which one of their stores were to be found. How old could he, Onoda, be at the time he utilized his last slug?

Lubang, Jungle Periphery

1954

The stormy season is finished. The wilderness is steaming. A huge number of birds break out in celebration. The men overview the territory. Onoda filters the edge of the backwoods, where it goes over into open country. His field glasses have experienced throughout the long term, the sodden has gotten into them, and a smooth growth has spread over the focal points. Yet, even with the unaided eye he can see that the steers are near the edge of the wilderness, where a piece of new grass has been let stand. It is just on the furthest side of that that the rice paddies start. Shimada is glad that for once their prey has come to them, it implies the meat will not need to be hauled up to this point.

There is one cow nibbling under ten yards from the wilderness fringe. The warriors, very much covered up, keep still. Without moving, they study the environmental factors. There is nothing strange. Shimada, at long last, fretful, leaves the haven of the thick foliage and approaches the cow, his rifle evened out at her head. Then, at that point, the situation becomes ridiculous. Fire from different sides; a painstakingly arranged snare. Slivers of twigs fly up from the brambles where the shots are coming from. Shimada twirls around to return fire, yet at that exact second he is struck in the head. He drops like a felled tree trunk. Onoda and Kozuka fire away fiercely. In a frenzy two or three Filipino warriors flee. One of them is hit by Onoda, and hauled once again into cover by his companions. Onoda's rifle jams, and he can't fire. Yet, the adversary is as of now pulling out. After a concise second's thought, under covering fire from Kozuka, Onoda surges up to Shimada, however a look is sufficient to let him know he's previous assistance, he's dead. Angered, Onoda

aimlessly fires into the thick wilderness the adversary has
removed into.

Lubang, West Coast

1971

26 years now after the finish of the conflict. Another sunrise breaks over the island. The sun disconnects itself from the skyline in a flare of red and orange. Striations of downpour loom over the marshes. Weird bugs go creeping up the wilderness lianas, difficult to tell what they're about. Onoda notices B-52 aircraft high overhead, leaving their fourfold fume trails. Onoda is currently beyond fifty, and more surrendered, more unemotional than any other time in recent memory. The coast here is dark volcanic stone, blended with little sandy sea shores. Behind it the mountains rise steeply, canvassed in wilderness. The real coast is perilous, presented to see from all over. Onoda is lying on his back, Kozuka is mounting watch. Onoda gives him the field glasses. North of one eye, the focal points are less thoroughly congested with growth.

Onoda is persuaded that this is another age of planes, which they have been noticing now starting around 1966 or somewhere in the vicinity. The groups of them are getting bigger constantly. "Americans?" asks Kozuka.
Onoda is in not even a shadow of a doubt, despite the fact that he can't see the blazons from such a long ways beneath. "From Clark Air Base?" theorizes Kozuka, however Onoda is dubious. "It's unrealistic for such weighty planes to rise so steeply over such a brief distance. Apparently these are from Guam." That would likewise be the sensible clarification for the shift of the battlefield toward Southeast Asia or India. Made his thought process of India?
"India," makes sense of Onoda, "has liberated itself from the British, and Siberia has parted away from Russia. They have

now joined Japan, to shape a strong triple union against America." Kozuka is fretful. They had spent unreasonably lengthy here presented to see. Onoda orders a fast retreat up into the precarious jungled slants.

A resting place in the main part of the wilderness. Birdsong, enraged mosquitoes. The two men are standing, squeezed near one another. Onoda, in fact gifted, has long presumed that this new age of airplane no longer purposes propellers. Given the height they fly at, they should have the option to fly a lot quicker than any propeller pivot could accomplish.
"Why?" asks Kozuka.
"Since the air gets so dainty up there that a plane can remain airborne provided that it flies very quickly." Onoda holds out a container evenly to exhibit the standard: there should be a shut chamber in which the fuel is scorched violently, with an opening at the back. The set energy free from the blast powers the chamber forward, similarly as a nursery hose would pull back from its opening in the event that one didn't clutch it.
"In any case, how could it be that the blast or progression of blasts doesn't annihilate the chamber and the plane?" asks Kozuka.
"A vehicle does likewise — huge number of blasts each moment in the inside of the motor without obliterating it," Onoda controls him. It was his expectation that one of these planes could crash-land on Lubang, and offer him a chance to assess one of these fly motors.

Lubang, Hill 500

1971

Onoda and Kozuka are progressing. Each step they take is cautious and slow. They keep inside the front of the wilderness until they arrive at the uncovered highest point of Hill 500. Something is different here. Then, at that point, they see it, a little card table has been set up, with a thick roll of paper on it enclosed by plastic. A sign has been put in the grass. It peruses "News from Japan" in Japanese characters. Onoda and Kozuka keep their eyes on it until it gets dim, not until the next morning do they dare leave the security of their disguise. Onoda cautiously bumps the roll all around with the gag of his rifle, prior to taking it in his grasp. A paper, for sure, newly printed. It has been here two days and no more; somebody probably been up here preceding them. Hastily the two warriors pull out into the safe house of the wilderness.

Not until they get to the Looc Overlook, from where it is feasible to see foe developments far off, do they hurl themselves upon their find, pore over the paper centimeter by centimeter. Onoda turns it over, sees promotions for electrical kitchen gear, for vehicles, for lipstick. He turns around to the first page title: Australia and New Zealand are finishing their association in the conflict. A further segment: the disastrous South Vietnamese hostile in Laos. Beneath it a photo, with warriors frantically sticking on to an American helicopter flying out the injured. How could America be supporting Vietnam? Onoda ponders. Has the battlefield moved farther West, as he finished up quite a while back, or has Laos presently joined India, China, and Siberia in the new enemy of American partnership? Kozuka believes it's conceivable. Onoda, however, stays far fetched, and puzzles over whether the paper isn't a fraud from the American mystery administration. For what reason didn't he consider that immediately? However, Kozuka focuses to the little promotions, which look pretty veritable to him. Onoda turns over the pages over and over, lastly establishes that the foe has accessed a real paper, and just messed with specific pages. A few significant things, Kozuka notices, were totally ignored, like Japan's part in this conflict. What's more, the numerous segments of promotions are a preferable option over shutting down entire pages. "Beside the first page," Onoda ascertains, "close to a portion of the print surface comprises of notices. Yet, papers have never doled out more than a few percent of their space for publicizing. Nobody will at any point purchase everything, that is totally unimaginable. They've controlled the genuine news, and supplanted it with publicizing."

Kozuka's consideration is again attracted to the first page, which is dated March 19, 1971. This is conclusive, definitive proof of distortion for Onoda: the release is originated before. "Today is March 15; the blockheads don't have any idea how to appropriately count."
"However, imagine a scenario where — " Kozuka objects.
Onoda takes a gander at him pointedly. "What if what?"
"Imagine a scenario in which our schedule wasn't exactly correct," says Kozuka, "simply assuming."
"It is," Onoda guarantees him, "I worked in all the jump years, I've noticed the moons — "
"The moon can play stunts," says Kozuka.
Onoda reflects. "Right. The lunar stages are not useful in making a schedule, and when we were on the run, I wasn't generally ready to monitor the days. Likewise, on the grounds that we're so near the equator here, it's hard to precisely gauge the late spring and winter solstices. In any case, even with all that, I actually know how to count."

"I am sorry, Lieutenant," says Kozuka.

Obscurity has fallen. The two men keep on gazing at each line, each photo, each promotion. A little fire gives adequate light, they hold the paper straight up to their countenances, their heads appear to sparkle from the fire. Something is annoying Onoda. He tunes in. Nothing. Then, at that point, he freezes, goes after his rifle.
"Something's happening," he murmurs.
Kozuka hunches down, strains his ears. However at that point Onoda finds something that could give off an impression of being the most normal thing on the planet, yet to him it is an outright sensation.
"See, there's Looc. They have power." And certainly, the town that is small is enlightened by some neon tubes, a fantastic event. The two fighters haven't seen power for perhaps five years, the last time was in Lubang municipality, from a good ways. Onoda accepts they are in for a few harder times now, particularly around evening time, when the foe can turn on extraordinary searchlights and search for them. Kozuka simply needs to see the value in the change.

The next day, Onoda makes one more disclosure through his misted field glasses. Six ranchers are working out in the open, however they are joined by two men in civilian clothes who are conveying rifles. Not troopers, obviously, yet guards, watching them while they work. How to respond? Onoda settles on an assault. It's been excessively since a long time ago they've exercised authority over.

Lubang, the Lowlands close to Looc

1971

Onoda and Kozuka are leveling themselves through lengthy grass, sneaking forward in the way of a lioness moving toward her prey. A couple of palms, a few papayas in among them. The laborers are snickering as they work.
"Where are the two guards?" murmurs Onoda.
Kozuka spots them. "Left-hand side, you can simply see them under the material sunroof."
Onoda strains his ears. "I can hear music."
"A radio? How could a radio work out here in the open?"
Kozuka murmurs. Onoda chooses to assault. He leaps out, starts shooting. The laborers shout, escape this way and that. One of the guards attempts to discharge a fired, however obviously his firearm isn't even stacked. Different peppers away in the overall course of Onoda, yet just catches up with stones on the ground that go skittering, however one shot kicks back and hits Onoda in the foot. After an hour, he will acknowledge he has seeped into his boot. The field has been cleared by its safeguards. Kozuka snatches a sack of rice, a cleaver, a couple of papayas. Onoda takes the little shortwave radio that is as yet playing music from the neighborhood station. The voice of a Tagalog-speaking DJ is spreading careless cheerfulness. The speaker is genuinely feeble, and at first Onoda can't track down the off button. He would rather not offer their situation as they retreat.

"Desde la Capital del Tango, desde Buenos Aires," Onoda hears from the amplifier whenever he at last has an opportunity to search for a station in the security of a concealing put under a stone projection. How might it at any point be within the realm of possibilities to get Buenos Aires, a portion of a world away?

ponders Kozuka. As far as himself might be concerned, Onoda is entertained at what Kozuka was educated at school. These were shortwave signals that are shot up to the stratosphere and afterward skipped around to different regions of the planet. Since the volume is so low and hauls, Onoda dismantles the thing, and closes the batteries are practically drained. In any case, something different astonishments him. This radio has no cylinders, so there probably been some unprecedented development. He wipes the batteries and returns them to. A ton of static, pieces of different dialects, and afterward out of nowhere, for under a moment, the peak of a Beethoven piano sonata. Then, at that point, a Japanese station. Since the volume is so weak, and the gathering goes back and forth, the two men press their ears to the little amplifier, and their heads lie together. A horse race is being communicated.

"Also, presently," the radio speaker reports, "the second occasion of the night, the Kyoto Grand. The most loved is Cherry Blossom, the female horse . . ."

"Six furlongs, mind blowing, I can scarcely recollect what a pony resembles," murmurs Kozuka.

"What's more, evidence," boasts Onoda, "that Japan is doing very well in the conflict. Do you suppose they'd arrange horse races in any case?"

The gathering continues to remove, yet it is without a doubt a race meet. "What's more, presently Pride of Hokkaido . . . starts to lead the pack, the field is fanned out on the last straight . . ."

Since the batteries are so frail, Onoda warms them in his armpits.

"Here is the game plan for race number four: Plumed Arrow, Bird of Prey, White Shadow, the previous victor of the Tokyo Open, skipping tensely . . ."

"We could wager on the victor," proposes Kozuka.

"I have to take a hard pass, I don't understand anything about these racehorses of yours," Onoda objects. Kozuka gestures.

However at that point Onoda has a shift in perspective. "Great, I bet on White Shadow, he seems like a victor."
Kozuka plumps for Bird of Prey. However, the amplifier has an unexpected coming up for them.
"Gracious, no, no, no, NO," goes the pundit's voice. "White Shadow has broken out of the beginning box and has tossed his rider. White Shadow with void seat, crosses the track and makes for the vehicle leave. Stable chaps are in pursuit, yet how might they track down the steed among 20,000 left vehicles? Presently the race should start without him."
"20,000, unimaginable," mumbles Kozuka.
"Once when I was on the track," Onoda reviews, "there were a ton of transports and perhaps 200 vehicles. Not more."
Then, at that point, grinning, he makes an idea: "In the event that you accurately pick the victor, that would address your prevalent knowledge, and you could be my supervisor for one day."
A few times the two men draw spaces, however at that point, in one race that is basically imperceptible, Kozuka wagers on Samurai Number One. The name is barely referenced, however unexpectedly the short of breath analyst goes: "Shinjuku has the lead, yet is hailing severely. All of a sudden, Samurai Number One floods forward. He has come straight up from the back, presently he's ahead of the pack, it's endlessly neck. Samurai Number One is the champ by a short head."
Onoda praises Kozuka on his triumphant nature. The following day Kozuka is the pioneer, however he has no clue about how to manage his advancement. Throughout the long term, his subordinate job has so come to characterize him that he is not really in that frame of mind to give a straightforward order. However, the men chuckle about it, and it turns into a somewhat happy day of minor setbacks. Since the batteries are now spent, Kozuka recommends — an idea, not a request — going after Lubang municipality, to get more.

"Kozuka," comes Onoda's devastating rejoinder, "you are my chief today, however we can't go after Lubang. We would need to cross a few kilometers of open level ground, and Lubang has by my evaluation 800 occupants. Presumably more."
"Sorry," swallows Kozuka. "Indeed, it was only a thought."

Lubang, the Lowlands near Looc

1971

Onoda and Kozuka are evening out themselves through extensive grass, sneaking forward in the method of a lioness pushing toward her prey. Several palms, a couple of papayas in among them. The workers are chuckling as they work.
"Where are the two gatekeepers?" mumbles Onoda.
Kozuka spots them. "Left-hand side, you can basically see them under the material sunroof."
Onoda strains his ears. "I can hear music."
"A radio? How should a radio work over here in the open?" Kozuka mumbles. Onoda decides to attack. He jumps out, begins shooting. The workers yell, get away from all over. One of the watchmen endeavors to release a terminated, but clearly his gun isn't even stacked. Various peppers away in the general course of Onoda, yet finds stones on the ground that go skittering, but a single messed kicks back and catches up with Onoda. Following 60 minutes, he will recognize he has saturated his boot. The field has been cleared by its shields. Kozuka grabs a sack of rice, a knife, several papayas. Onoda takes the little shortwave radio that is at this point playing music from the local station. The voice of a Tagalog-speaking DJ is spreading thoughtless liveliness. The speaker is really weak, and at first Onoda can't find the off button. He would prefer not to offer their circumstance as they retreat.

"Desde la Capital del Tango, desde Buenos Aires," Onoda hears from the speaker whenever he finally has a valuable chance to look for a station in the security of a disguising put under a stone projection. How should it anytime be possible to get Buenos Aires, a part of a world away? considers Kozuka. Taking everything into account, Onoda is engaged at what Kozuka was instructed at school. These were shortwave signals that are shot up to the stratosphere and a while later skipped around to various districts of the planet. Since the volume is so low and takes, Onoda destroys the thing, and shuts the batteries are basically depleted. Regardless, something else amazements him. This radio has no chambers, so there likely been some phenomenal turn of events. He wipes the batteries and returns them to. A lot of static, bits of various lingos, and a short time later all of a sudden, for under a second, the pinnacle of a Beethoven piano sonata. Then, a Japanese station. Since the volume is so frail, and the get-together goes this way and that, the two men press their ears to the little enhancer, and their heads lie together. A horse race is being conveyed.

"Additionally, as of now," the radio speaker reports, "the second event of the evening, the Kyoto Grand. The most cherished is Cherry Blossom, the female pony . . ."

"Six furlongs, mind blowing, I can barely remember what a horse looks like," mumbles Kozuka.

"Also, proof," flaunts Onoda, "that Japan is doing very well in the contention. Regardless, do you guess they'd organize horse races?"

The social event keeps on eliminating, yet it is point of fact a race meet. "In addition, as of now Pride of Hokkaido . . . begins to stand out, the field is spread out on the last straight . . ."

Since the batteries are so fragile, Onoda warms them in his armpits.

"Here is the strategy for race number four: Plumed Arrow, Bird of Prey, White Shadow, the past victor of the Tokyo Open, skirting rigidly . . ."

"We could bet on the victor," proposes Kozuka.

"I need to take a hard pass, I see nothing about these racehorses of yours," Onoda objects. Kozuka signals.

Anyway by then Onoda has a change in context. "Extraordinary, I bet on White Shadow, he appears to be a victor."
Kozuka plumps for Bird of Prey. Be that as it may, the intensifier has an unforeseen coming up for them.
"Benevolent, no, no, no, NO," goes the intellectual's voice. "White Shadow has broken out of the starting box and has thrown his rider. White Shadow with void seat, crosses the track and makes for the vehicle leave. Stable chaps are in pursuit, yet how should they find the horse among 20,000 remaining vehicles? As of now the race ought to begin without him."
"20,000, impossible," murmurs Kozuka.
"Once when I was on the track," Onoda surveys, "there were a lot of transports and maybe 200 vehicles. Not more."
Then, smiling, he makes a thought: "If you precisely pick the victor, that would address your predominant information, and you could be my boss for one day."
A couple of times the two men draw spaces, but by then, in one race that is essentially subtle, Kozuka bets on Samurai Number One. The name is scarcely referred to, but startlingly the winded investigator goes: "Shinjuku has the lead, yet is hailing harshly. Out of nowhere, Samurai Number One floods forward. He has come straight up from the back, as of now he's in front of the pack, it's unendingly neck. Samurai Number One is the champion by a short head."
Onoda acclaims Kozuka on his victorious nature. The next day Kozuka is the trailblazer, but he knows nothing about how to deal with his progression. All through the long haul, his subordinate occupation has so come to describe him that he isn't exactly there of psyche to provide a direct request.
Notwithstanding, the men laugh about it, and it transforms into a fairly cheerful day of minor misfortunes. Since the batteries are presently spent, Kozuka suggests — a thought, not a solicitation — pursuing Lubang region, to get more.

"Kozuka," comes Onoda's overwhelming reply, "you are my main today, but we can't pursue Lubang. We would have to cross a couple of kilometers of open level ground, and Lubang has by my assessment 800 tenants. Apparently more."

"Sorry," swallows Kozuka. "For sure, it was just a thought."

"That is so a lot," wonders Kozuka.

Onoda raises his shut clench hand. "Furthermore, for what reason does the item explore over the two Poles, and at an even speed? Every upheaval of the earth takes it somewhat more than 60 minutes, a fantastic speed."

Kozuka attempts to keep up: "And why over the North and South Poles?"

Onoda gets a straight twig and fastens it in an upward direction in his clench hand, so that a little stands out under and on top. "Envision this is the pivot of the earth."

He gradually turns his clench hand. The article flies over the South Pole, is gone from sight, returns over the North Pole, and turns. Presently, this is the basic thought: with every revolution, the earth has turned somewhat farther so that each time, the item follows its course over an alternate section of the earth. Like an orange, when you strip it and you see the fragments. In the event that it is perpetually flying from one Pole to another, the article will before long have a perspective overall planet, section by portion."

"Furthermore, what might be the benefit of that?" asks Kozuka.

"Battle, obviously. War," Onoda answers without hesitation. "To assemble such an article is a phenomenally muddled endeavor and would be so expensive cash that it must be for some tactical reason. It very well may be a review stage for the whole planet, section by portion, or it very well may be an epic bomb. It very well may be exploded voluntarily over any spot on the planet. One can drop it on Mexico or Antarctica, on our Lubang. No put on earth is protected any more."

Before long, the men make another disclosure, considerably more dull this time, on their wilderness pathway close to 500: it is a Filipino magazine destroyed. As Onoda carefully flicks at the worn out remainder with the tip of his recently gained blade — he is opposed to contact the actual pages — the two men see explicit pictures. Unusually wound stripped bodies, performing unchaste demonstrations in gatherings, in miserable setups. Kozuka had no issue with taking the piece with them, however Onoda allows it to lie where he saw it, in case the adversary, who had forgotten about it as snare, comprehend that they had passed along these lines.

Lubang, Hill 500

1971

From inside a tangled bramble, Onoda and Kozuka view peculiar improvements on the uncovered culmination. A temporary street has been laid through the wilderness to the pinnacle. Trucks, laborers in hard caps, a group of assessors, two convoys set next to each other obviously comprising an impermanent arranging community. The most striking component is an iridescent yellow Caterpillar earth mover from the United States. Away somewhere out there stacked up mists are jerking with quiet lightnings. Kozuka hypothesizes on the development of an exceptionally huge ordnance base, yet what are the goals reachable for weapons situated up here? Also, where are the fighters to safeguard the laborers? Through his destroyed field glasses, Onoda takes a good look at the territory farther down, and finds a group of around fifty Filipino troopers progressing gradually in a lengthy record toward the edge of the wilderness. A fighter each two or three yards or so demonstrating to Onoda that this is no genuinely compelling military move; in the real wilderness they would need to be a lot nearer together. Such a battue must be successful with 1,000 men along a whole kilometer. In the entirety of his time opposing, Onoda still can't seem to see sniffer canines being used, and even sniffer canines wouldn't have a potential for success against furnished men. You can get unarmed men with canines, and the Philippine Army appears to have gotten a handle on that. As may be obvious, the inadequate equal development is only another sign that the warriors are excessively reluctant to enter the wilderness.

The two men are investing always of their energy in the maintenance and fixing up of their hardware. The mugginess perplexes everything, everything decays, conflicts, disintegrates.

At the point when they do their week by week clothing in security, it begins to rain, and they need to stash their half-dry dress in a plastic sack. It rains the following day, and the following, and when it's dry once more and radiant, they find their plastic sack siphoned up like an elastic inflatable going to explode. All that in it is white and loaded with fine strings, it looks like a haze of sugar candy from a youngsters' fair, however what it is a shape that has multiplied fiercely.

Onoda is chipping away at his jeans, which he needs to fix with some material that in variety anyway a similarity to the material of his unique uniform. Kozuka in the interim is winding around a rattan net that he needs to fasten to the highest point of his backpack.
"Why is that," he asked, "does the Lieutenant want an almost identical type of his uniform? For what reason does it need to look legitimate?"
"Are we officers or drifters?" Onoda answers harshly.
A little plane surprises them, it has all the earmarks of being circumnavigating. They run mindfully to where they can see better. The single-motor plane flies in sluggish circles, then, at that point, one of the side entryways is taken out and supplanted by an enormous amplifier.
"Lieutenant Onoda," says a voice in Japanese, "Confidential Kozuka, this is an enticement for you" — however at that point it takes a couple of additional circles before the men have heard the whole message — "an allure for you from the President. Emerge from your concealing spot, you are guaranteed of a reprieve."
"Babble, that is another snare," Onoda announces. "Why send an entire force of men against us simultaneously?"
Kozuka feels quite skeptical of his own. "President? Leader of what? Of the Philippines? Also, provided that this is true, then, at

that point, shouldn't something be said about America? Or on the other hand does he mean the President of the USA?"
The structure site on Hill 500 appears to recommend some incredible holding between the fighting Americans and the Filipinos.

Lubang, Jungle Footpath

October 19, 1972

Yet again on the track, this time moving in reverse. Onoda stops abruptly on the grounds that the bird babble has halted. He plunges into the thick foliage, Kozuka stows away next to him. They see something shiny sparkling on the way. It is by all accounts a touch of tinfoil, similar to the piece they tracked down the other week, with a couple of scraps of chocolate on it. Kozuka pulls himself up to make an assessment.

"Pause," murmurs Onoda, yet Kozuka is now out of cover. The tinfoil begins rippling toward him, like a blast had happened, however it is gunfire. Yells, wild developments, slugs destroying leaves. Then quiet. Kozuka is remaining in the way.
"Chest," he says tranquilly, like conversing with himself, "It's my chest."
His breath comes whistling, blood rises at his mouth, and he flounders down look ahead.

Lubang

From late 1972

Onoda, for the following two years or few seconds, is a moving around piece of the wilderness. On one event, detecting he can never again move of a running segment of Filipino troopers, he speedily covers himself in foliage, sprinkles leaves over himself at the last seconds. In his scramble, a stray strides on his hand without taking note.

An open air fire. Crickets. Mosquitoes. Endlessly downpour. Onoda is feeling reflective. He severs mussels from the stones on the stony West coast. He gets a fire going in the way of the lumberjacks, he abandons no follow. He assumes he has been neglected, yet one day he sees a few men beneath Looc Overlook. One of them is conveying an amplifier on his back like a backpack, his face is clouded from sight as he strolls down the slope. The voice calls out in Japanese: "This is your sibling, this is your sibling. I'm your sibling Toishi."
Onoda goes inflexible.
"Hiroo, my sibling," refers to the voice as, "pay attention to me." Onoda appears without feeling, his inside is stone. The incomprehensible can't be.
"My kin, come out any spot you are, arise, arise." The voice withdraws into the distance, can be heard hardly.
Onoda strains everything in himself to follow it.
"I will sing a melody currently," calls the far off voice, "Hiroo, my sibling, do you recall the tune we used to sing at cherry bloom time?"
Onoda simply gets the initial bar of the tune, from there on the wilderness brings the voice into itself.
"See the falling blooms, they are the spirits of the dead, they sail through the air . . ."

What was that? Was that really his sibling, or some dim fabrication? Onoda can't represent the occasion in that frame of mind of his conviction. He is compelled to live with the inconsistency. In the event that it really was his sibling, for what reason does he hear the voice for quite a long time and all around the island? The response attracts him perpetually capably: on the off chance that that was his sibling out with a pursuit party, he was telling him, so to talk in a mystery code, that the men were really entrusted with investigating everywhere of Lubang to make a definite geographical review for further developed guides to work with the unavoidable reconquest of the island by the Imperial Army. Truth accompanies stowed away codes, or probably the codes are eccentrically advanced with the real world, similar to the veins of mineral in rock.

As of now, time stops still for a really long time. Or on the other hand rather, it doesn't stop, it essentially does not happen anymore. Then, at that point, it hustles, jumps over long stretches of time at the time it takes a breeze to mix the leaves. Onoda circumvents like a sleepwalker, however even that is certainly not a genuine impression. He harbors two qualities. Onoda goes around watchfully, sees everything, hears everything. He is constantly ready. Yet, he isn't permitted to be wilderness, be a piece of nature only. He is separated and a section. He should help the general population in Lubang to remember his main goal, so he ventures out from the shadows on the northern plain external Lubang municipality, and discharge a couple of shots high up. There is nobody there. He has compelling reason need to take more supplies. He simply needs to make himself understood.

Lubang, Wakayama Tributary

Walk 9, 1974, 8:00 a.m.

A Japanese banner is fluttering over an enormous tent. Enormous enough for a man to stand up inside it. Next to it is Suzuki's more modest tent. Onoda is all around secret by the rushlike grass at the intersection of the two streams. He is still. Nothing, no Filipino fighters, no columnists, there is obviously no trap. Suzuki comes creeping out of his tent, and starts cleaning his teeth, he is precisely above Onoda, whom he has not seen. "Try not to move," says Onoda smoothly, pointing his rifle at the rear of Suzuki's head.

"Onoda," says Suzuki, "Hiroo Onoda."

"You have stayed faithful to your promises, whatever they may be. Pivot."

"I have accompanied your chief from Tokyo," says Suzuki, talking into the mouth of the rifle, "Major Taniguchi."

"Furthermore, in any case?"

"No other person. A unit of the Philippine first class Army Corps is anticipating you on Hill 500."

"Furnished?" asks Onoda.

"Indeed, however just trying to give you respect as a praiseworthy gatekeeper."

"Where is my boss?" Onoda is careful. "I should accept there is some snare."

"Major," refers to Suzuki as, "would you compassionately step outside. Lieutenant Onoda is here."

Be that as it may, the Major doesn't arise, he hasn't got his boots on yet. Onoda stands and holds up next to the mouth of the enormous tent. Inside, hands mess with the opening. Taniguchi ventures out, an elderly person, white haired and stooped, 88 years of age.

"Lieutenant," he says, "I remember you. You have turned into a developed man."

Onoda salutes, makes two strides back, and presents arms.

"Do you remember me?" asks Taniguchi.

"Indeed, sir." Onoda secures.

"I have new requests for you from the Ministry of Defense."
Taniguchi isn't in uniform, simply a military shirt and the crested
cap of the Special Forces. He holds a piece of paper in his
lengthy hands and peruses from it. "According to the Emperor's
rules, the Fourteenth Army and any excess Japanese units have
shut down a wide range of fight. Units under the order of the
Special Forces are thusly to stop threats forthwith. They are to
put themselves under the order of the Philippine powers, and
adhere to their directions."

Onoda is very unconcerned. He salutes.

"Lieutenant, your conflict is finished." Because Onoda has gone
unbending, Taniguchi presently requests him in a generously
tone from voice: "Lieutenant, would you say you are okay?"

Onoda's unfilled face double-crosses nothing, he appears to be
gone to stone. Emotionlessly, he answers: "Sir, there is a
whirlwind seething inside me."

"Lieutenant, calm," says Taniguchi. "For the prosperity of the
construction, I ought to include that this request is significant as
of now, generous 800 hours, March 9, 1974."

Onoda abruptly drops to the floor, like drained to the rear of the
knees. The Major is perturbed. "What is wrong, Lieutenant?" But
Onoda is unequipped for discourse.

"Won't you say something," mumbles Taniguchi.

"In the event that today is March 9," says Onoda distrustfully,
I'm five days behind with my retribution."

"You are 29 years behind," Taniguchi revises him.

On the manner in which up to Hill 500, Onoda requests pass on
to make a diversion. He needs to bring his blade from its
concealing spot in the tree empty. His blade is in great condition,
without a hint of rust. The sun sparkles on the sheath. As late as
possible, Onoda is later to trust, he has trusted that the Major will

go to him and let him know that this has all been a touch of theater, they had just needed to test his constancy.

Lubang, Hill 500

Walk 9, 1974, 10:30 a.m.

The exposed ridge has changed. The recently assembled radar station is coming to fruition. A first class unit of the Philippine Army is on march. Taniguchi is first to venture out from the dark, trailed by Onoda. An official barks a request, and the unit presents arms. Onoda takes the investigation, precisely, like this must be a deception. Toward as far as it goes stands the General in by and large order of the Philippine military. Onoda moves forward to him, salutes, gives up his rifle. Then, at that point, he surrenders his sword also, in both expanded hands, however the general gives it back to him right away. "The genuine samurai keeps his sword," he says. Onoda has long felt unequipped for feeling, however later he will concede that inside all that in him was wailing.

And afterward this: not long after Onoda's re-visitation of Japan, Norio Suzuki embraced his endeavor to the Himalayas to track down the sasquatch, as he had planned. At the foot of Dhaulagiri, he is struck by a torrential slide and killed. Hiroo Onoda immediately flew from Japan to Nepal. Joined by a Sherpa, he set off on the three-week journey and moved to a level of 5,000 meters, to the superb southern flank of the 8,000 meter top. Where Suzuki lay covered, the Sherpas had fabricated a cairn. Onoda's carrier put down his backpack. "This is the grave here." Onoda had the impression of tremendous clench hands descending upon him from the sky, like the boundless idea of the blanketed pinnacles, the icy masses, the abysms would tear him in two. Onoda moved forward to the cairn. The main hint of the existence that had been was a vacillating petitioning heaven banner. As unconcerned as everything around him, Onoda remained to consideration. The mists separated momentarily, a

modest look at daylight. No seismic tremor, no thunderclap.
Quiet.

After Onoda had given up to the Philippine powers, he was taken
by helicopter to Manila. Ferdinand Marcos, recently introduced
as President yet governing by military regulation, pursued the
open door of having the acquiescence of the sword reenacted as
a media scene. He, as well, returned the sword immediately. On
his directions, Onoda had placed on his worn out uniform,
despite the fact that he had been given another suit of non
military personnel garments on Lubang. Marcos declared a
pardon for Onoda because such an extremely long time he had
been a foe warrior. Individuals of Lubang themselves had taken
Onoda for a foe specialist of some kind. Years after the fact, he
returned there for a little while, and was generally welcomed by
local people. Be that as it may, the question of those he had
killed among the populace never entirely disappeared.

At the point when insight about the finish of Lieutenant Onoda's
lone mission arrived at Japan, the hearts of a whole country
stopped.

As far as concerns him, Onoda, welcomed by a media scrum,
was profoundly upset by the realism of post bellum Japanese
society. As far as he might be concerned, it was like Japan had
lost its spirit. The Prime Minister needed to get him immediately,
however Onoda declined. He believed that initially should meet
the groups of his fallen companions. Afterward, he moved to
Brazil, where his more established sibling, Tadao, had moved,
got wilderness in the distance free from Mato Grosso do Sul, and
began his own cows farm. He spent piece of every year in his
country, where he began the Onoda Nature School, a
confidential foundation at which throughout the late spring
months he educated camps of schoolchildren in strategy for real
life adaptations. Onoda wedded two years after his return. He

had no youngsters. He kicked the bucket in Tokyo at the age of
91.

Onoda long wouldn't acknowledge trooper's compensation for
his 28 years. Just when squeezed by his family did he at long last
acknowledge the cash, giving it immediately to the Yasukuni
Shrine. There, from the mid-nineteenth hundred years, the names
of the now 2.5 million individuals who had lost their lives for the
country were kept. (Oddly, likewise the names of a portion of
their homegrown creatures.) The sanctum is a fairly disputable
organization since it likewise houses the names of around 1,000
sentenced war lawbreakers. From the start, I wondered whether
or not to follow Onoda's greeting. He needed to show me the
leftovers of his worn out uniform, which was kept there. As
Onoda had been formally proclaimed dead in 1959, there had
been no indications of something going on under the surface
from him for quite a while, and it was expected that he had
passed on in a similar trap in which Shimada had been killed or
that he had been mortally injured like Kozuka, his name had
been enrolled there for a long time. It required fourteen days of
discussions among Onoda and the top of the sanctum before I
was welcomed. I acknowledged the greeting, thinking who am I
at any rate to permit myself the advantage of such reservations,
coming as I do from a country that has brought such detestations
upon different nations and people groups. Onoda and I
immediately struck up a relationship. We figured out something
worth agreeing on in our discussions since I had worked under
troublesome circumstances in the wilderness myself and could
ask him inquiries that no other person asked him. Onoda had a
tune deciphered for me that he had remained quiet about singing
on Lubang, to keep his spirits up:

Calm moon, I might seem to be a drifter or bum,
In any case, you are observer to the magnificence of my spirit.

We stooped inverse the abbot in a long service. Petitions to God were said, then, at that point, the abbot went to me. What he said was deciphered for me, however I have no memory of any of it. At last, the abbot sent a priest from the room. He returned, conveying a level container got with silk strip. Inside was Onoda's uniform, pressed in crepe in the way of valuable articles of clothing. The crepe was painstakingly lifted aside, and it was right there, the uniform that Onoda had worn for quite some time in the wilderness, patched over and over. Onoda inquired as to whether he would allow me to take the uniform in my grasp. I bowed, and the abbot laid it in my officially outstretched arms. The abbot traded a couple of words with Onoda, and urged me to unfurl the uniform and to feel it. I did as such with intense consideration. As I did, I could feel something by the belt. Onoda saw, and gestured to me. I found a minuscule earthy colored glass bottle, of the sort that drug specialists use for prescriptions. It contained palm oil that Onoda himself had made. He hadn't understood that such countless many years after the fact, it was as yet secret in his uniform. I felt an uproar close to me. Onoda hadn't got to his feet, something had pulled him upstanding. That large number of present, still kneeling down, feeling a similar wound to the heart, showed homage him.

How is it that he could have failed to remember the jug? Something genuine that was kept secret some place separated from his recollections. Frequently he had contemplated whether the years in Lubang might have been long periods of sleepwalking, yet on the off chance that some substantial item that didn't show up in his fantasies out of nowhere emerged, then, at that point, he could never have been in a fantasy all things considered. What denotes the start of something obvious, and where could its memory be? Why, he frequently asked himself, would it be able to be that his unending wilderness walk was a deception? After the entirety of his great many advances, he had perceived that there was — there could be — no such thing as the present. Consistently was past, and each further step was future. The raised foot was past, a similar foot put in the mud before him still ahead. Where was there space for the present? Each centimeter of his foot proceeding was the future, each centimeter behind was past. Etc, in increasingly small scope, in millimeters, in scarcely quantifiable parts of millimeters. We assume we embrace the here and now, however there is nothing of the sort. Am I strolling, living, battling? And afterward shouldn't something be said about every one of those stretches when he had strolled in reverse, to hoodwink the adversary? Indeed, even his retrogressive step was a stage into what's in store.

The past could constantly be estimated and portrayed, yet his memory had obscured occasions, at times bewilderingly stirred them up. Indeed, even 10 years after Shimada's demise he kept on seeing him in the wilderness ahead. His memory had not stretched out its elegance to the safeguarding of agony. (Any other way ladies would barely consent to bear more youngsters after the torment of labor.) what was to come was consistently similar to a misshaping yet impervious haze lying over a new scene, however there was some information on it. The day is finishing. The sun will ascend toward the beginning of the day. The blustery season will start in five months. And afterward the unforeseen, the surprise out of nowhere: a projectile, similar to a crease of tracer in the gloaming. It will hit you, on the off chance that you don't figure out how to turn to the side without a second to spare. The point that it would have struck, the sunlight based plexus, is no longer where it was. The rot of his uniform is unavoidable, however certainties can in any case be kept away from, or possibly postponed. Each fix eases back the crumbling, the wear, the decay. Toward the end it was as yet a uniform.

After the visit to the place of worship we talked in the recreation area until sunset. Is it true or not that he was then a sleepwalker, or was currently, the present, something he had imagined? He frequently thought hard about the inquiry on Lubang. There was no confirmation that when conscious he was alert and no verification that while dreaming he was dreaming. The nightfall of the world. Insects, when they stop, for reasons unknown we don't have the foggiest idea, move their recieving wires. They have second sight. Crickets shout at the universe. Among the dread of night was a pony with sparkling eyes, smoking stogies. A holy person left a profound engraving on the stone on which he rested. Elephants around evening time dream standing up. Fever dreams trundle the stone of night up the irate bubbling mountains. The wilderness twists and stretches like caterpillars strolling, uphill and down. The heron when cornered will go after the eyes of its followers. A crocodile ate a noblewoman. The dead, when gotten some distance from the sun, can covered stand up. Three men on a pony, the seat stays vacant. The net of the resting angler keeps on getting fish. A man who strolls in reverse ought to likewise talk in reverse. Onoda in reverse is Adono. The core of a hummingbird beats twenty times each second, twelve hundred times each moment; the quiet Indios in the Mato Grosso do Sul accept they are alive two times. It is just among his cows in the Mato Grosso that Onoda has a good sense of safety. His heart beats with their souls, his breath goes back and forth with theirs. At the point when he is with them, he realizes he is where he is. The night is finished, and the multitudes of fish don't know anything.

In 1997, I was in Tokyo to coordinate the show Chushingura. Shigeaki Saegusa, the author, had long squeezed me to assume the world debut of this work. Chushingura is the most Japanese of every single Japanese story: there is a strict service looming; the arrangements are close by; throughout these, a medieval ruler is incited and offended; he draws his blade. As discipline for his blasphemy, he is made to commit custom self destruction, seppuku. After two years, 47 of his retainers retaliate for him by ambushing and killing the one who offended their lord. They realize that they should bite the dust for such an activity. That very day, every one of the 47 commit suicide.

Saegusa is a generally regarded writer in Japan. At the hour of the creation, he had his own TV show, and individuals had some awareness of the work we were doing. At night, a few of us would eat together at a long table. Saegusa arrived behind schedule one day, and in a condition of high fervor. "Herzog-san," he said. His Highness, the Emperor had demonstrated he would get me to a confidential crowd, in the event that I wasn't excessively occupied with the forthcoming debut. I answered: "wow, I have no clue about what I would discuss with the Emperor; it would be only trivialities." I could feel my significant other Lena's nails diving into my palm, yet it was past the point of no return. I had declined.

It was a blooper, so terrible, so devastating that I wish right up to the present day that the earth had gobbled me up. Around the table, everybody present froze. Nobody relaxed. Everyone's eyes were fixed on their plates, nobody took a gander at me, an extended quiet made the room shiver. It felt to me like the entire of Japan had quit relaxing. All at once, into the quiet, a voice asked: "All things considered, on the off chance that not the Emperor, whom might you want to meet?" I in a split second answered: "Onoda."

"Onoda? Onoda?"

"Indeed," I answered. "Hiroo Onoda." And after seven days, I met him.

www.ingramcontent.com/pod-product-compliance
Lightning Source LLC
LaVergne TN
LVHW011047200726
843509LV00011B/1362